797,885 Books
are available to read at

Forgotten Books

www.ForgottenBooks.com

Forgotten Books' App
Available for mobile, tablet & eReader

ISBN 978-1-332-77848-5
PIBN 10443506

This book is a reproduction of an important historical work. Forgotten Books uses state-of-the-art technology to digitally reconstruct the work, preserving the original format whilst repairing imperfections present in the aged copy. In rare cases, an imperfection in the original, such as a blemish or missing page, may be replicated in our edition. We do, however, repair the vast majority of imperfections successfully; any imperfections that remain are intentionally left to preserve the state of such historical works.

Forgotten Books is a registered trademark of FB &c Ltd.
Copyright © 2015 FB &c Ltd.
FB &c Ltd, Dalton House, 60 Windsor Avenue, London, SW19 2RR.
Company number 08720141. Registered in England and Wales.

For support please visit www.forgottenbooks.com

1 MONTH OF FREE READING

at

www.ForgottenBooks.com

By purchasing this book you are eligible for one month membership to ForgottenBooks.com, giving you unlimited access to our entire collection of over 700,000 titles via our web site and mobile apps.

To claim your free month visit:

www.forgottenbooks.com/free443506

* Offer is valid for 45 days from date of purchase. Terms and conditions apply.

English
Français
Deutsche
Italiano
Español
Português

www.forgottenbooks.com

Mythology Photography **Fiction** Fishing Christianity **Art** Cooking Essays Buddhism Freemasonry Medicine **Biology** Music **Ancient Egypt** Evolution Carpentry Physics Dance Geology **Mathematics** Fitness Shakespeare **Folklore** Yoga Marketing **Confidence** Immortality Biographies Poetry **Psychology** Witchcraft Electronics Chemistry History **Law** Accounting **Philosophy** Anthropology Alchemy Drama Quantum Mechanics Atheism Sexual Health **Ancient History Entrepreneurship** Languages Sport Paleontology Needlework Islam **Metaphysics** Investment Archaeology Parenting Statistics Criminology **Motivational**

Screens and Galleries in English Churches

BY

FRANCIS BOND

M.A., LINCOLN COLLEGE, OXFORD; FELLOW OF THE GEOLOGICAL SOCIETY, LONDON
HONORARY ASSOCIATE OF THE ROYAL INSTITUTE OF BRITISH ARCHITECTS
AUTHOR OF "GOTHIC ARCHITECTURE IN ENGLAND"

*ILLUSTRATED BY 152 PHOTOGRAPHS AND
MEASURED DRAWINGS*

HENRY FROWDE
OXFORD UNIVERSITY PRESS
LONDON, NEW YORK, AND TORONTO
1908

PREFACE

IN the last years before the Dissolution, when the English churches had become all glorious within, what first arrested and what detained the attention above all the rest was the soaring Rood and Rood screen, silhouetted against the splendid glass of the great east window of the chancel. No church was so humble but had its Rood and Rood screen. These form the subject of the present volume. As in his larger work on the *Gothic Architecture of England*, it has been the aim of the writer to present the subject from an evolutionary point of view. The story, therefore, commences with the Rood and Rood beam of the early Christian churches; it follows their gradual development on the one hand into the chancel screen of the parochial and collegiate churches, on the other hand into the quire screen and rood screen of the churches of the monks and the regular canons. Finally it traces to the transposition of the rood lofts the galleried churches of the seventeenth and eighteenth centuries. It is a story of growth and development conditioned by doctrinal and ritualistic changes spread over sixteen centuries.

In the preparation of this volume, in addition to valuable assistance from many friends, and from the literature generally which has accumulated on the subject, the writer is under special obligations to the various papers by Mr F. Bligh Bond, which form, indeed, the *locis classicus* on the subject of screens, and the contents of which will be embodied shortly in a larger work. Mr W. Davidson also has generously permitted the use of his unpublished notes and drawings of the screens of Norfolk. For the revision of the proofs, grateful acknowledgments are due to Mr Aymer Vallance, Rev. G. W. Saunders, and Mr W. Davidson. Most of the screens have been visited, and several have been photographed by the writer; but the wealth of illustration here presented could never have been brought together but for the willing and generous co-operation of very many photographers and ecclesiologists, among whom special mention must be made of the members of the Architectural Detail Postal Club; in all cases specific acknowledgment is made in the *Index Locorum*, page 183.

The present volume will be followed shortly by one on "Fonts and Font Covers." Descriptions and photographs of important and interesting examples will be welcome; they should be addressed to Francis Bond, Stafford House, Duppas Road, Croydon.

TABLE OF CONTENTS

CHAPTER I

ORIGIN OF SCREENS - - - - - - - PAGE 1

CHAPTER II

CHANCEL SCREENS AND GALLERIES IN PARISH CHURCHES
    Plan of Screens - - - - - - -
    Presbytery Screens - - -
    Parclose Screens - - - - - -
    Stone Screens - - - - - -
    Oak v. Stone Screens - - - - -
    Construction of Oak Screens - - - -
    Cost of Screens - - - - - -
    Inscriptions on Screens - - - - -
    Design in the Screens of East Anglia and the West of England
    Paintings on Screens - - - - - -
    Welsh Screens - - - - - -
    Foreign Influence - - - - - -
    Chronology of Screens - - - - -
    The Rood - - - - - - -
    The Rood Beam - - - - - -
    The Rood Loft and its Uses - - - -
    Tympanic Screens - - - - - -
    The Commandments - - - - -
    Royal Arms - - - - - - -
    Tower Screens - - - - - -
    Destruction of Screens - - - - -
    Galleries - - - - - - -
    Dorset Music - - - - - -

CHAPTER III

QUIRE SCREENS IN CATHEDRALS AND COLLEGIATE CHURCHES   151

CHAPTER IV

QUIRE SCREENS AND ROOD SCREENS IN CHURCHES OF MONKS
    AND REGULAR CANONS - - - - - 157
    The Quire Screen or Pulpitum - - - - - 159
    The Rood Screen - - - - - - - 161
    Fence Screens - - - - - - - 165

MEASURED DRAWINGS - - - - - 166-181

INDEX LOCORUM - - - - - - - 183

INDEX RERUM - - - - - - 191

BIBLIOGRAPHY

BARTON TURF, NORFOLK. "Illustrations of the Screen." Rev. John Gunn. Norwich, 1869.
BLOXAM, M. H. "Gothic Architecture," ii., iii.
—— *Assoc. Societies Reports*, xii. 176.
BOND, F. BLIGH. "Screens and Screenwork in the English Church." *Journal of R.I.B.A.*, Part I. in 3, xi. 537; Part II. in 3, xi. 637.
—— "Devonshire Screens and Rood Lofts." *Proceedings of Devonshire Association*, xxxiv. 531.
—— "Screens near Minehead, Somerset." *Somerset Arch. Soc.*, lii. 55.
—— "Screenwork in the Churches of North-East Somerset." *Somerset Arch. Soc.*, liii. 82.
—— "Mediæval Screens and Rood Lofts." *St Paul's Eccles. Soc.*, v. 197.
—— "Winsham, The Tympanum as Surviving in." *Somerset Arch. Soc.*, xlix. 56.
—— "English Church Screens and Rood Lofts—their Origin and Development; with a full descriptive list of West Country Screenwork," and "a Special Study of the Figure Panels," by Dom Bede Camm. To appear shortly.
CAMM, DOM BEDE. "Devonshire Screens." 1905.
COX, Dr J. C., and HARVEY, A. "English Church Furniture." 1907.
DAVIDSON, W. (Owen Jones Student, R.I.B.A.). Unpublished notes and coloured drawings of Norfolk screens.
DUNCAN, LELAND E. "Parish Churches of West Kent, their Dedications, Images, and Lights." *St Paul's Eccles. Soc.*, iii. 241.
ENLART, CAMILLE. "Manuel d'Archéologie française," i. Paris, 1902.
FERRY, B. "Rood Screen of Christchurch, Hants." *Arch. Journal* v. 144.
FLEURY, ROHAULT DE. "La Messe," iii. 105-133, and Plates 239-246.
FOX, F. F. "Roods and Rood Lofts." *Bristol and Gloucester Arch. Soc.*, xxiii. 79.
FOX, G. E. "Notes on Painted Screens and Roofs in Norfolk." *Arch. Journal*, xlvii. 65.
—— "Victoria History of Norfolk," ii. 547.

FRITTON, SUFFOLK. "Illustrations of the Screen. Rev. Richard Hart. Norwich, 1872.
GALPIN, F. W. "Old Church Bands and Village Choirs." *Dorset Field Club*, xxvi. 172.
HEMS, HARRY. Lecture to Society of Architects on "Rood Screens." &c. 21st April 1896.
HENFREY, H. W., and WATNEY, H. "East Anglian Rood Screens." *British Arch. Assoc.*, 37, 135.
"HIERURGIA ANGLICANA." New edition. 2 vols. London, 1902.
KEYSER, C. E. "List of Mural and Painted Decorations." Third edition. 1883.
—— "On the Panel Paintings of Saints on the Devonshire Screens." *Archæologia*, lvi. 183.
—— "On the Wenhaston Doom." *Archæologia*, liv. 119.
"MONTGOMERY SCREENS AND ROOD LOFTS." Archdeacon Thomas. *Archæologia Cambrensis*, 6, iii. 96.
PUGIN, A. W. "Chancel Screens and Rood Lofts." 1851.
RANWORTH. "Illustrations of the Screen." C. J. W. Winter. Norwich, 1867.
SCHARFF, G. "Doom Picture in Gloucester Cathedral." *Proceedings of Society of Antiquaries*, III. 215.
SCOTT-ROBERTSON, Canon W. A. "On Kentish Rood Screens." *Arch. Cantiana*, xiv. 370.
SCOTT, Sir GILBERT. "The Choir Screen in Canterbury Cathedral." *Arch. Journal*, xxxii. 86. On the remains of Prior Eastry's work in 1305 on its eastern side.
SIRR, H. "The Stallwork, Canopies, and Rood Screens of the Fifteenth Century." *Art Journal*, 1883 and 1885.
SOMERS, CLARKE. "Sandridge Church." *Arch. Journal*, xlii. 247.
STRANGE, E. F. "Painted Rood Screens of East Anglia." *Architects' Magazine*, 1906, 105.
SYMPSON, E. MANSEL. "Lincolnshire Rood Screens and Rood Lofts." *Assoc. Societies' Reports*, xx. 185.
TARVER, E. J. "Screens." *St Paul's Eccles. Soc.*, iii. 16.
THIERS. "Traité des Jubés."
TUCKETT, F. F. "Notes on French Jubés." *Bristol and Gloucester Arch. Soc.*, xxv. 134.
VALLANCE, AYMER. "Mediæval Rood Lofts and Screens in Kent." *Memorials of Old Kent*, 1907.
—— "Roods, Screens, and Lofts in Derbyshire Churches," in *Memorials of Old Derbyshire*, 1908.
WALKER, D. "Rood Screens and Timber Work of Powys Land." *Powys Land Club*, iii. 211, iv. 181, vii. 61.
WARREN, R. H. "The Choir Screen in Bristol Cathedral." *Bristol and Gloucester Arch. Soc.*, xxvii. 127.
"YORKSHIRE, CHANCEL SCREENS OF." By Rev. C. B. Norcliffe. Giving particulars of the destruction of Yorkshire screens under the direction of the Dean of Ripon in 1720. *Assoc. Societies' Reports*. vi. 177.

BEACON TOWER IN SOUTH WALL

STONE ENGRAVING OF THE CRUCIFIXION.

THIS stone engraving of the Crucifixion, with a curious ornamented border, is probably of the latter part of the 12th century, and with the possible exception of part of the Font, it is the oldest carved work now remaining in the Church. It is built into the wall over the organ keyboard, where it was brought in 1899 from outside the South Door of the Nave.

On the South Wall opposite are the early English Sedilia. The window above them is of the date of the early 15th century. The monument on the right of the window is to Sir Thomas Spert, 1541. He was Comptroller of the Navy to Henry VIII., and founder of the Corporation of Trinity House. On the left of the Sedilia is the monument of Sir Benjamin Kenton, 1800. He was originally a potman in Aldgate, but became a wealthy man, and a liberal benefactor to many charities.

SCREENS AND GALLERIES IN ENGLISH CHURCHES

CHAPTER I

ORIGIN OF SCREENS

FROM the earliest times, as soon as ever a Christian church was built, the apse or sacrarium, in which in primitive days was the only altar which the church possessed, was protected by some kind of fence. Of these enclosures of the altar the first that we hear of are railings of wood or bronze. The Church of the Apostles, erected by Constantine at Constantinople in the fourth century, had its sanctuary divided off by a "reticulated screen of gilded bronze." The sanctuary of the Church of Tyre, built by Bishop Paulinus, was surrounded "*cancellis ex ligno ?fabricatis,*" i.e., "by wooden railings." St Germanus, Patriarch of Constantinople, speaks of the Holy of Holies as being accessible to priests only, and being fenced off by bronze railings. Of such railings, however, no examples survive.

Old St Peter's

In such examples as survive, the altar rails take quite another

Rome, St Clement's

Rome, St Maria in Cosmedin

form, viz., that of a colonnade. Immediately in front of the altar is an open colonnade of slender marble columns carrying an entablature, *e.g.*, at Old St Peter's, Rome (1).* How ancient these colonnades may be it is not possible to say; they may possibly go back at least to the sixth century. The lofty colonnade doubtless had some points of superiority over the earlier rail-fence, otherwise it would not have been adopted. What these points of superiority were, however, can only be stated conjecturally. One probably was that lamps could be suspended from it, and also curtains or veils to shroud the altar from view at penitential seasons; another, that on the beam or entablature could be placed basins or candlesticks containing lights; also reliquaries; and, above all, a cross, or later a crucifix, flanked by images of the Blessed Virgin and St John Evangelist. These were important practical advantages. Of them we shall probably be right in regarding the support of the cross or the rood as the primary and most important. This is borne out by the fact that a rood beam is known to have been in existence in Old St Peter's, Rome, in early days; it was of silver, and was presented by Pope Leo III. (795-816). We may fairly conjecture that, being of or plated with silver, there existed earlier still plain rood beams of wood. Now, the greater churches of the early Christians were all unvaulted, and the nave, and consequently the chancel arch or Arch of Triumph, was exceedingly broad. A rood beam of wide span, unsupported, would certainly have sagged at the centre. To prevent this, supports would be added, and these supports would naturally take the form of columns, as at Old St Peter's. This was to convert the rood beam into a rood screen. Such an erection was at once altar railing and rood screen.

Then came a change in church planning. In the earliest churches the apse was attached directly to the nave, and formed a sanctuary, containing the high altar. A quire was also needed, and for the purpose of a quire the western bays of the nave were appropriated. Just as the altar had been fenced off by railings or by a colonnade, so the quire needed to be enclosed and secured from intrusion. This was effected by erecting round it a wall or parapet, which was kept quite low, so as not to block the view of the altar. These quire enclosures usually consisted of thin marble slabs, about 4 feet high. The slabs were sometimes solid, but covered with carved work, especially with interlacings, *e.g.*, at St Clement's, Rome (2), frequently they were pierced, as at Torcello. Of these marble enclosures

* See plan in *Gothic Architecture in England*, 147.

of the quire many still survive, some going back to the sixth century, viz., those of St Clement* and St Maria in Cosmedin, Rome (2), and that of St Jean, Monza.* Other well-known examples, many of them of rare beauty, may be seen in Torcello and Ancona Cathedrals, the Museum at Brescia, St Mark's, Venice,† and elsewhere. Even so late as the fire of 1174, a low wall, a lineal descendant of the low early Christian parapets, survived in Canterbury Cathedral, on either side of the quire. For Gervase, the monk, says that "at the base of the pillars was *a wall of marble slabs*, which, surrounding Ernulph's quire and presbytery (built 1096-1115), divided the church from its sides, which are called *alæ*." ‡ In St Maria in Cosmedin (2) both arrangements are seen, a colonnade in front of the altar and a low parapet enclosure round the choir.

The next step is to consolidate both these, and to make the combined colonnade and western parapet occupy the position of the western parapet. This is well seen at Torcello in the Venetian lagune (5), where the cathedral was rebuilt in 1008, with fittings of earlier date brought from the mainland. Here the colonnade is not in front of the sanctuary, but three bays west of the sanctuary arch or Arch of Triumph; and its bottom part consists of a low parapet.

But, not later than the ninth century, in many churches a great change of plan had come in. This was to elongate the apse westward for two bays or more; in other words, to arrange that the eastern limb of the church should henceforth include space not merely for the apse, but for the quire as well; and the quire, instead of occupying the western bays of the nave, was now placed in the western bays of the eastern limb.§ This

* Illustrated in Cattaneo's *Architecture in Italy*, Figs. 8 and 11.

† Cattaneo gives a seventh-century example from St Mark's, Venice; eighth-century examples from Athens Cathedral, Cividale, Albenga, Modena Cathedral, &c.; several examples of the ninth century from basilicas in Rome; and numerous examples of the eleventh century. Illustrations are given in *La Messe* of the screens of St John the Evangelist, Ravenna, fifth century; St Sophia, Constantinople, sixth century; St Nicholas, Myra, sixth century; St Nicodemus, Athens; Torcello Cathedral; Sion, ninth century; Mount Kasbek, Caucasus; Jouarre, France, ninth century; see Plates 240-245.

‡ What is seen now at Canterbury is the parclose screen put up by Prior Eastry, *c.* 1305; the base of it, however, is that of a parclose screen of masonry which, from its mouldings, must have been put up *c.* 1175, *i.e.*, by William of Sens, which again superseded that of Priors Ernulph and Conrad described by Gervase.

§ There were, of course, "survivals" of the older arrangement; no great church in England put the stalls into the eastern limb, till that of Canterbury was rebuilt *c.* 1200; and in some cases the stalls remain to this day in the eastern bays of the nave, *e.g.*, at St Albans and Westminster.

ORIGIN OF SCREENS 5

change is seen quite clearly in the plan drawn out in the ninth century for the Benedictine Church of St Gall.* In such a church the stalls could be placed in the eastern limb, and the colonnade parapet could be placed at the entrance to the eastern limb, effectually guarding quire and altar at once. Quire screens of this colonnade type persisted here and there abroad till the

Torcello Cathedral

eleventh century and later at Torcello, St Mark's, Venice, and elsewhere.

But, it may be urged, quire screens in England were never of the classical type of columns and entablature, at any rate not till the English Renaissance gave us such examples as the

* Illustrated in *Gothic Architecture in England*, 194.

6 SCREENS AND GALLERIES

Reculver

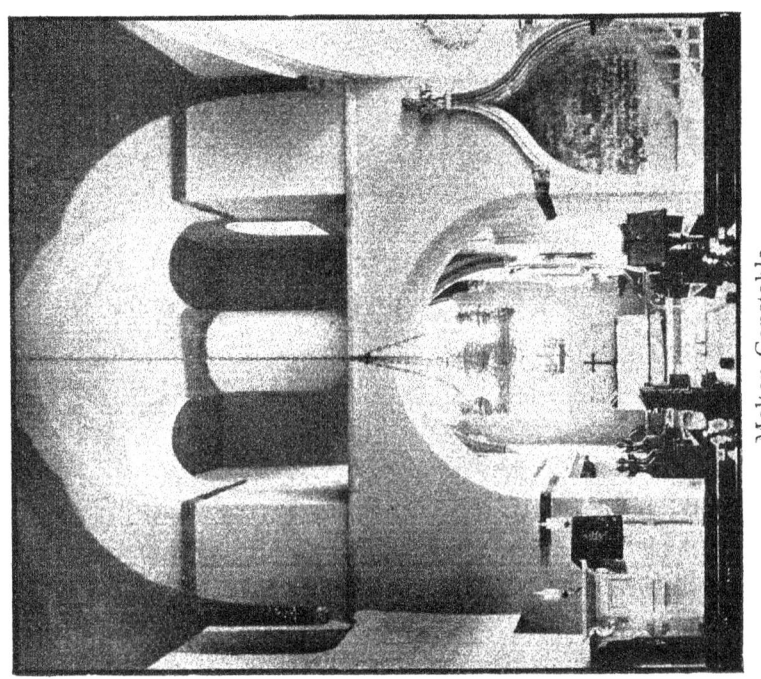

Melton Constable

screens at Washfield and Stonegrave. But this is not so. We really had once screens of the colonnade type; and what is very important, they occurred in the earliest English churches of which we have any remains. For the triple chancel arches of the earliest Anglo-Saxon churches are nothing but a deliberate attempt to reproduce, more or less faithfully as material served, such colonnade screens as that of Old St Peter's, Rome. These triple chancel arches occur very frequently in the very earliest churches that we possess, viz., the small group that were built in the seventh century. Remains of one have been found at Brixworth, Northants; sketches of a triple chancel arch at Reculver, Kent, before the church was pulled down in the nineteenth century, are extant; there are the remains of another at St Pancras, Canterbury; and evidence that triple chancel arches existed at St Peter-on-the-Wall, Bradwell, Essex, Rochester, and Lyminge; in fact the presence of a triple chancel arch in an Anglo-Saxon church at once raises a strong presumption of seventh-century date. Now the arches at Reculver (6) rested on columns; and these columns, though the arches have been destroyed by a vandal vicar, still exist; for they were transferred to Canterbury, where they have been re-erected north of the north transept of the cathedral.* In the ruined Church of St Pancras, behind the Canterbury Hospital, there is evidence of the existence of a colonnade of four Roman shafts reused; the base and the lower portion of the southernmost of these are still *in situ*. Not every Anglo-Saxon church, however, in the seventh century would be able to borrow for re-erection ancient Roman shafts and columns; it is not surprising, therefore, that in the remaining examples the triple chancel arch rests, not on columns, but on piers. But whether the supports be piers or columns, the triple chancel arch may, with much probability, be regarded as a lineal successor in design to such a colonnaded screen as that of Old St Peter's. After the seventh century it is replaced in Anglo-Saxon work by a single chancel arch.

After this it is not known with certainty to appear till the thirteenth century.† But in the end it was superseded by

* Whether these columns are Anglo-Saxon imitations of Roman work, as is the opinion of Mr G. E. Fox, or Roman work reused, as Professor Baldwin Brown inclines to believe, is "*nihil ad rei*": in any case they are columns.

† There are, indeed, semicircular triple chancel arches, *e.g.*, at Ovingdean and Pyecombe, Sussex, and at Credenhill, Herefordshire, of Norman character; but in the first two instances at any rate the lateral arches are known to have been cut in recent times. In other instances the lateral arches may be but lateral altar recesses, such as those at Eartham, Sussex (27), cut down to the ground in recent times. Triple chancel arches

the single chancel arch combined with a screen, loft, and rood—a combination difficult to obtain with the obstructive central piers or columns of a triple chancel arch.

How early screens within a single chancel arch appeared in England it is impossible to say. Canterbury Cathedral possessed one at any rate not later than the early years of the twelfth century. Earlier still, in the previous century, we have evidence at Bury St Edmunds of a rood; and if a rood, a rood beam also. It was given by Archbishop Stigand.* It is true that this rood was placed over the high altar and not beneath the chancel arch; but we may be sure that if roods and rood beams existed over high altars, they existed also in the more normal position at the entrance to the quire. Not much later we hear of a rood "apud Winchelcumbam." William of Malmesbury, lib. iv. 323, says that a flash of lightning "trabem maximam perculit, ut fragmina in tota spargerentur ecclesia; quin et crucifixi caput cum dextera tibia et imaginem sanctæ Mariæ dejecit"; *i.e.*, it broke up the rood beam, splintered the image of our Lord, and hurled down that of the Blessed Virgin; this was on 15th October 1091. Here then also there were both rood and rood beam; and the latter doubtless would in time, if it had not them from the first, receive supports, and be converted from a rood beam into a rood screen.

Summing up, we conclude that the origin of the mediæval quire screen is twofold. Partly it is to be found in altar fences, whether railings or colonnades, partly in low parapets forming quire enclosures; both parapet and colonnade being ultimately combined in one, and placed at the entry to the chancel; of such an arrangement the triple chancel arch of the seventh-century Anglo-Saxon churches may be regarded as a survival. Partly it is to be found in the necessity of providing supports for a rood beam, which should carry a cross or crucifix, lamps, reliquaries, curtains, &c. The rood beam with its supports developed in Italy into a colonnade; in England into the quire screen of oak or masonry.

are not definitely known to recur till the thirteenth century; and we can hardly regard the occurrence of these triple arches, after a disuse extending through six centuries, as a survival of the seventh-century Anglo-Saxon use. Thirteenth-century examples occur at Wool, Dorset, and Westwell, Kent. Fourteenth-century examples at Capel-le-Ferne, Kent; Bottisham, Cambridge; Great Bardfield and Stebbing, Essex; Bramford, Suffolk; other late examples occur at Baginton, Warwick, and Compton Bassett, Wilts.

* "Crux erat super magnum altare, et Mariola et Johannes, quas imagines Stigandus archiepiscopus magno pondere auri et argenti ornaverat, et sancto Aedmundo dederat" (*Cronica Jocelini*, 4).

Other accounts, however, of the origin of the mediæval quire screen have found favour. It is pointed out that throughout the Greek and the Latin churches, it was of primitive usage to draw veils round the altar so as to hide from the people the act of consecration—a usage, which in the Greek church has crystallised in the Iconostasis, a lofty screen of solid stone behind which consecration always take place. It is noteworthy that in Italy this usage always remained in vogue; a ciborium or baldachino being erected over and around the altar, between whose pillars were rods on which curtains could be drawn.* There is definite evidence as to the use of veils in our own Pre-Conquest churches. Bloxam quotes words from an ancient Anglo-Saxon pontifical, "*extenso velo inter eos et populum*"; *i.e.*, a "*veil was stretched between priests and people*"; which implies that if veils were not stretched round the altar, they were placed across the chancel arch, which in the early Anglo-Saxon churches was usually quite narrow. Even in the thirteenth century the tradition of the demarcation by veil was not extinct, for Durandus, writing on Symbolism, mentions it as an alternative to demarcation by a screen of masonry: "interponatur velum aut murus inter clerum et populum." There are, however, serious objections to regarding the quire screen as a substitute, either for the veils of a baldachino, or for the Lenten veil. As for the first, the quire screen does not occupy the position of the altar veil. As for the Lenten veil, it is true that in a parish church it covered the western side of the quire screen. But in the greater churches it did not; *e.g.*, the position of the winch still remaining shows that at Salisbury it occupied a position intermediate between the quire screen and the high altar. What is more important—it never did, as a matter of fact, become a substitute for the Lenten veil—every church possessed a quire screen and a Lenten veil as well. Such a hypothesis as to the origin of the quire screen may safely be set aside.

Another origin has been suggested. In the early Christian basilicas there was on either side of the arch of the sanctuary an ambo or pulpit. Many of these survive. From these ambos were read the epistle and gospel. They may still be seen used for that purpose in Italy, *e.g.*, in Milan Cathedral, and in nearly every cathedral of Spain.† On the strength of this usage it has

---

* This led to a remarkable divergence between Italian and Transmontane ritual. In Italy, the altar being already screened by the veils of the baldachino, there was no need to put up a quire screen; the absence of quire screens therefore bringing about a vast difference in the appearance of the interiors of the churches of Italy and those across the Alps.

† In Spain they are sometimes of metal, *e.g.*, in Toledo Cathedral.

been thought that the mediæval quire screen is but a pair of early Christian ambos connected by a platform. But in England, at any rate, there is no evidence for the use at any time of ambos. Moreover, abroad, when ambos were employed, the reader turned to the west; in England, when the gospel or epistle was read from the loft of a quire screen, the reader turned to the east. Finally, there is no satisfactory evidence that there was a loft in any of our churches, at any rate in the parish churches, before the fourteenth century; and in any case, the explanation is applicable only to the loft, and not to the screen.

Whatever its origin, the screen was of great practical use. One reason for its continuance and popularity is worth setting forth somewhat at length. From the earliest times the English parish church seems to have possessed at least three altars. Now it was a custom in England to make the chancel, even in the humblest parish churches, narrower than the nave. Why? It involved a good deal of extra trouble with quoins, and some extra expense. The reason probably was that it was desired to place two of the three altars, one on each side of the chancel arch. The altars did not need to be of great length; square altars were quite common. The more the chancel arch was narrowed, the more room there was for these side altars. This may be the reason why the tradition of a small doorway-like chancel arch, such as that of the Anglo-Saxon church at Bradford, Wiltshire, continued here and there through the Norman period on into the thirteenth century. But an arch so narrow was an obstruction to the view of the third altar, the High Altar. The remedy was to widen the chancel arch, but to put an open-work screen in front of it. This allowed at once a fair view of the high altar, while it also provided a backing or reredos for the two side altars. That such side altars did exist is no mere conjecture; some may still be seen *in situ*. At Peterchurch, Hereford, cn the borders of Radnor, there is still an altar slab on each side of the apse. The little church of Patricio, Brecknock (78), far up in the Black Mountains, retains two altars in front of the screen, one on either side of the central door of the choir screen; two more remain at Urishay. Two side altars are recorded to have stood in Llangwm Church, Monmouth. At Hauxton, Cambridge, is a narrow chancel arch, flanked by recesses, in which there were side altars, *c.* 1229. At Tattershall, Lincolnshire, in a screen presented in 1528, are two side recesses; each side recess has on the south side a piscina, so that there can be no doubt that each recess contained an altar. On the painted panels of the screen at Strumpshaw, Norfolk, are marks showing where side altars stood. The famous screen at Ranworth, Norfolk has wings designed as reredoses to side altars. There are, moreover many examples of chancel arches with a recess in the wall on either side; *e.g.*, at South Shoebury, Essex, Melton Constable (6), and Castle Rising, Norfolk; in this last, a Norman church, the northern recess is semicircular, the southern one has been pointed in Gothic days.* Later on, usually not till the thirteenth or fourteenth century, aisles were added to most churches, and the side altars would then usually be transferred to the eastern bays of the aisles, screened off for that purpose, in which there would be room for a fullsized altar slab. But quire screens did not for that reason cease to be put up; they had by now been found far too useful in other ways; moreover, it was no doubt already in contemplation to provide lofts, and screens were wanted to support them. The screen, therefore, was still retained; nor were the side altars always dislodged from their ancient position on either side of the screen door. The late Gothic reredos behind the pulpit of Chipping Norton† plainly proves that in this church, at any rate, the northern side altar of the screen was never removed.

* Illustrated in *Gothic Architecture in England*, 162.
† Illustrated in *Gothic Architecture in England*, 548.

Harberton

CHAPTER II

CHANCEL SCREENS OF PARISH CHURCHES

OF the artistic value of screens, even though they be, as in a little church at Haverfordwest, a rude framework of common deal, there can be no question. Nothing adds so much to that most potent of all effects in church architecture, "mystery," as a screen, with its vistas half hidden, half revealed, of beautiful and holy things beyond. "Keep," Wordsworth says—

> " Keep the charm of not too much ;
> Part seen, imagined part."

Nor does anything add so much to the apparent length of a church as to break it up with a screen; contrariwise, nothing diminishes the apparent length of a church so much as the removal of the chancel screen, as may be seen in many a church now too short and broad in proportion, *e.g.*, Louth,* Lincolnshire, or North Walsham ; or with a screen too thin and flimsy, *e.g.*, Tewkesbury and Durham.† Of this Pugin had no doubt, nor did he hesitate to express himself clearly on the subject. The man, he says, who professes to love Gothic architecture, and does not like screens, is a liar.

The parochial chancel screen takes three forms. In small churches it extends merely across the east wall of the nave; but in aisled churches it is often prolonged north and south across the aisles as well, if they terminate more to the east than does the chancel arch, *e.g.*, at Harberton, Devon (12). In late days sometimes, especially in East Anglia, the aisles are carried on for the whole length of the quire or of the presbytery eastwards. In such a church it is absolutely necessary to carry the screen across nave and aisles, in order to separate aisled quire from

---

* Illustrated in *Gothic Architecture in England*, 213.

† Moreover, without a screen and loft the glare of the huge east window, so characteristic of English church design, is simply intolerable. It was only when lofts and screens came into general use that it became possible to add such great increase of dimensions to the east windows of chancels.

14 SCREENS AND GALLERIES

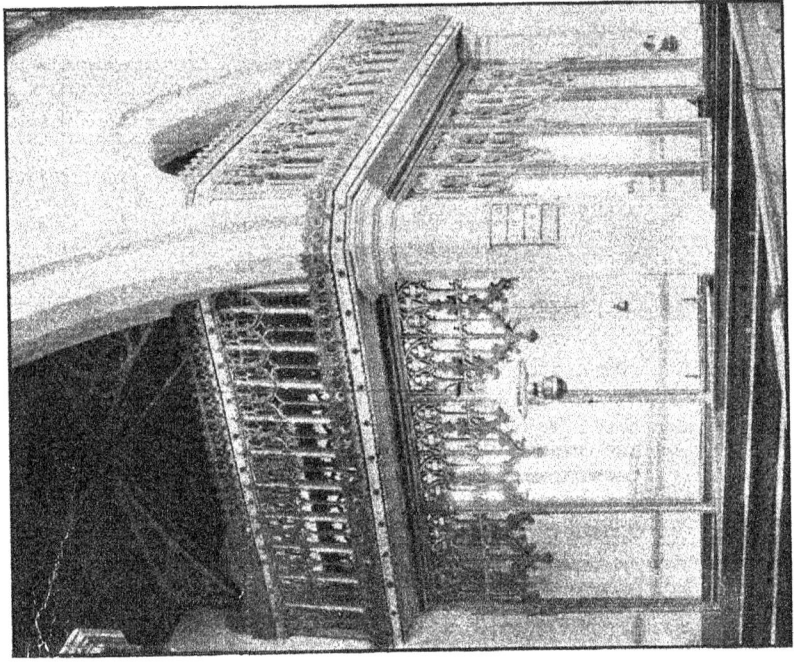

Denning on N.E. Chapel of Nave

Dennington, S.E. Chapel of Nave

aisled nave. In Cornwall and Devon, indeed, the normal type of late Gothic church is one in which the aisles extend along the whole length of the church. Sometimes they are lofty and broad; sometimes, instead of nave and lofty aisles, there are two or three parallel naves; or, as they are called in the indenture for making a rood loft at Stratton, "three *churches*." In these counties, therefore, and in the neighbouring county of Somerset and in East Anglia, chancel screens being so often a necessity received greater development than anywhere else in England. One leading reason for this was the change in the planning of parish churches (the only important change since the twelfth century) which came in first perhaps at North Walsham, Norfolk, when that great church was rebuilt after the damage done by the Peasant Revolt of 1381. This change was to omit the chancel arch, *i.e.*, to make nave and chancel consist simply of one great unbroken hall.* In such a church, of course, a chancel screen was indispensable; without it, it would have been impossible to tell where the nave ended and the chancel began.

The screens of nave and aisles did not, however, always form one straight line as at Harberton. Sometimes a different arrangement had to be adopted. Very often there were no chancel aisles; the nave aisles terminated in a line with the chancel arch. In such a case the chancel screen could not be continued to the aisle walls. But it was customary to use the end bays of the nave aisles as altared chapels. When these, then, were screened off to the west and at the sides, the screens assumed quite a new plan; instead of being in a straight line, they ran, if one started from the south, to the north, east, north, west, north. This arrangement, except for the loss of the central screen and its loft, is perfectly preserved at Dennington, Suffolk (14); where, supposing that one ascended the loft by the staircase in the south aisle, one would first proceed round the south aisle chapel, then by the chancel screen across the chancel arch, and then round the north aisle chapel, descending by the staircase in its wall. In churches where the rood staircases are thus placed, *i.e.*, one bay west of the chancel arch, the above explains their arrangement.

In the West of England the screens were on a very large scale. The screens of Staverton (108) and Cullompton are continued across the aisles; the latter is 54 feet long, and retains all three doors; the former contains seventeen bays, and is 50 feet long and 15 feet high. One must see such Devon churches

* Noble examples of this treatment are to be seen at St Nicholas, Lynn; Gresford, Denbigh; many churches in Cornwall and Devon, and the modern church of St Agatha, Sparsholt, Birmingham.

SCREENS AND GALLERIES

Dunster

as Staverton, where not only the three screens are *in situ*, but the parapetted loft has been replaced; then restore in imagination, higher still, the great Crucifix with its guardians, and one may realise something of the ancient magnificence of the approach to the holy places of these village churches of England.

An exceptional arrangement occurs at Dunster, Somerset (16). The screen is a chancel screen running right across nave and aisles; but instead of being at the east end of the nave it is two bays to the west. The explanation is to be found in the fact that formerly the church was a monastic one, that of a cell* attached to the Benedictine Abbey of Bath. Over the nave the parishioners had certain ill-defined rights, which as usual led to quarrelling. In 1499 the matter was referred to the arbitration of the Abbot of Glastonbury, who apportioned the crossing and the quire to the monks, and the nave to the parish. To get a chancel, therefore, the parish erected a screen two bays west of the central tower; these two bays then formed the parochial chancel, and the parochial altar stood beneath the western arch of the crossing.†

Presbytery Screens

Screens were also employed in other positions than at the entrance to the chancel. Sometimes, though rarely, a presbytery screen is interposed between the sacrarium or presbytery and the quire. There is a light presbytery screen of open woodwork at St David's Cathedral (18). The presbytery screen of Brecon Priory is only known from an illustration. A few examples survive in parish churches, for instance at Michaelchurch and Brilley, Hereford. A presbytery screen at St Martin's, Colchester, consisting of a wooden arch carrying a cornice, is illustrated in Buckler's *Essex Churches*. In Postling Church, Kent, there are evidences of a narrow loft having run across the sanctuary, supported by two beams, but without a screen below; while the rood beam traversed the church at some distance to the westward.‡

---

* Its dove-cote and the prior's lodgings still survive in the neighbouring farm.
† Recently it has been removed to the eastern arch.
‡ *Home Counties Magazine*, July 1903.

St David's

PARCLOSE SCREENS

Lavenham

Astbury

Wolborough

Parclose Screens

Where there was an aisled quire, screens were necessary to shelter the clergy or monks during the long offices from the draughts in the unheated churches; as also to prevent the distraction which the movements of worshippers in the aisles and

Stamford St John

ambulatory chapels might cause to those in the quire. These must have been provided in quite early days. The monk Gervase describes low walls as fencing in Canterbury quire in the twelfth century. In the greater churches these parclose screens were usually of stone; Prior Eastry's screen at Canterbury is an example, as also Bishop Fox's screens at Winchester. Examples of side screens in oak are shown at Astbury, Cheshire (19), and Lavenham, Suffolk (19). In France the parclose screens have survived far more often than the western quire screen. Albi quire is enveloped all round by a magnificent screen of open work; solid screens, with niches on the outside crowded with statuary, survive at Amiens, Chartres, Toledo, and Burgos.

Very numerous parclose screens remain also round or in

East Harling

front of chapels; *e.g.*, the screens in front of the Lady Chapels of Ottery St Mary (37), and East Harling, Norfolk (22), and of the Chapel of St Mary Magdalen in Exeter Cathedral (35), and the oak screens round the chantry chapel of Wensley, Yorkshire. At Lavenham, Suffolk, two sets of late screens have been taken down and put together round family pews. At Wolborough, Devon (20), also, parclose screens are shown

STONE SCREENS

Capel-le-Ferne from West

Westwell from East

fencing a family pew. Screened chapels were most common, probably almost universal, at the east end of aisles; *e.g.*, at Dennington, Suffolk (14); Stamford St John (21); Brigstock, Northants; Walsoken, Norfolk (38); as may be seen by the very frequent presence of a piscina, proof of the existence of a former neighbouring altar. Sometimes the western as well as the eastern bays of the nave were screened off as chapels, as they are to this day at Addlethorpe, Lincolnshire (180).*

Stone Screens

Stone screens are comparatively rare in parish churches. In the first examples there is a triple chancel arch, *e.g.*, at Wool, Dorset, and Westwell, Kent (thirteenth century), (23), and Capel-le-Ferne, Kent (fourteenth century), (23), the three arches being equal in height, and pointed. Above them, resting on them, is solid wall carried all the way up to the gable.

In a variant of this, all this solid wall is omitted, except so much as occupies the spandrels of the three tall arches; practically it is reduced to a cornice, and the whole of the chancel arch is open from its springing to its apex. The screen consists of three arches with a horizontal finish. The fourteenth-century screen of Bramford, Suffolk (25), is an example; in this the spandrels of the arches are pierced with modern quatrefoils. Similar is the screen at Welsh Newton, Herefordshire (130). The screen at Bottisham, Cambridge (25), is a century later.

In another variant of this, the characteristic is, that instead of the three arches of Bramford, more are employed. Practically it consists of a cornice supported by more than three arches. The arches, being more numerous, are therefore narrower, and the effect resembles that of such an open oak screen as that of Lavenham or Southwold, except that in the oak screen the lower panels are solid. To this type belongs the beautiful screen at Bradford Abbas, Dorset (26), which, with the whole church seems to have been built in the latter years of the fourteenth century.

In the second type a different departure is taken. In many churches of all periods there are two openings, or "squints," one on each side of the chancel arch, *e.g.*, Eartham, Sussex (27). These were usually small; but sometimes they were large, and

* Measured drawing of the parclose screen at Luton in *Architectural Association Sketch Book*, v. pp. 56, 57; of those at Dennington in *Building News*, May 18, 1888; of the Ottery screen in *Exeter Diocesan Society's Journal*, i. p. 1.

STONE SCREENS

Bottisham

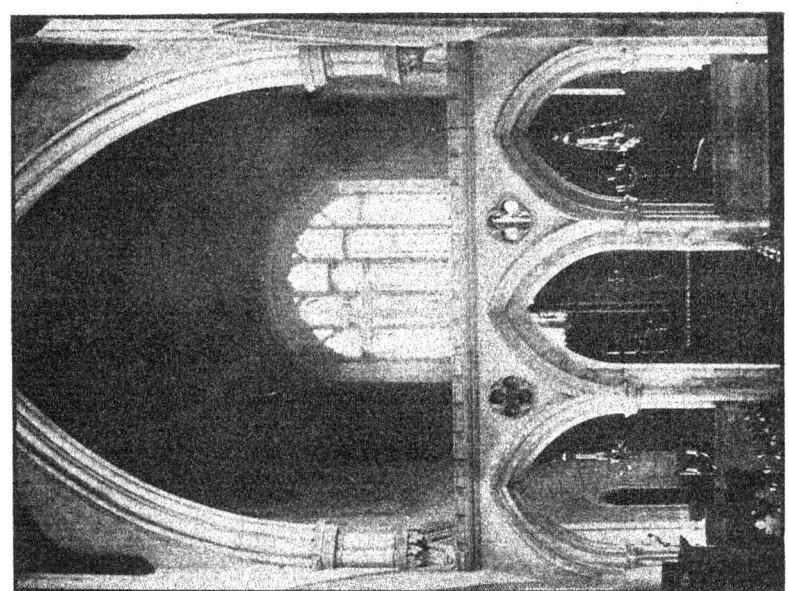

Bramford

D

were treated as unglazed windows, and were furnished with stone mullions and tracery. Such a design occurs at Baulking, Berks, Stockton, Wilts (27), and elsewhere. In such a case the screen consists simply of wall extending up to the gable, and pierced with a doorway and a couple of squints. A charming

Bradford Abbas

development of this type occurs at Brimpton, Somerset, where there is a stone screen with central door and low walls on either side. Each wall carries a low arcade of four open lancet arches. On the doorway and the light lancet arches is a cornice, the lower part which is of stone, the upper of wood. On the western

STONE SCREENS

Eartham

Stockton

sides of each low wall is a stone bench.* It is curious that these side squints sometimes occur on either flank of an oak screen, *e.g.*, at Patricio (78) and Swymbridge (61). They have been regarded as openings for reading desks, but such can hardly have been their purpose in a Pre-Reformation church. It has been suggested also that in front of each was fixed a movable retable or "table," but at Patricio the openings are not central to the back of the side altars, and for a retable it would be more

Sandridge

convenient to have a solid panel rather than an aperture. Sometimes a further step is taken; an unglazed window is inserted above the doorway; such is the design of Sandridge, Herts (28).† A variant is one in which there is only doorway, squints, and cornice, the wall being carried but little higher than the doorway, *e.g.*, Highway, Wilts.

* Illustrated in *Spring Gardens Sketch Book*, viii. 28.
† Illustrated paper in *Arch. Journal*, xlii. 248.

Great Bardfield

STONE SCREENS

Stebbing

In the third class the precedent of certain windows common at the end of the thirteenth and the beginning of the fourteenth century is followed; e.g., those of the clerestory of St Alban's, begun c. 1257, and the magnificent ranges of triplets in the aisles and clerestory of the quire of Milton Abbas, Dorset, rebuilt after the fire of 1309.* In this class the whole chancel arch is regarded as a single unglazed window. It is divided from the pavement to its apex into three lancet lights, of which the central one, the highest and broadest, runs up to the apex of the chancel arch, and has a lower and narrower lancet arch on either side. Sometimes another early fourteenth-century window is adopted as a pattern, e.g., that so common in Ottery St Mary's (begun in 1337), in which the mullions of the tall central lancet are carried straight up to the chancel arch, so that the central lancet is straight-sided.† Of the Milton Abbas design Stebbing, Essex (31), is a derivative; of the Ottery type, Great Bardfield, Essex ‡ (29). In both the rood, with its attendant figures, is combined with the "window screen" in most charming fashion.

A very extraordinary fact is the close resemblance of the great stone screen west of the Lady Chapel of Trondhjem Cathedral to that of Stebbing, Essex. The whole design from top to bottom would be perfectly at home in Ely, c. 1325. If such designs as those of Stebbing and Capel-le-Ferne be studied together, the conclusion is inevitable that the Trondhjem design is of English genesis. "That Trondhjem Cathedral was constructed by English architects, or at any rate by architects taught by Englishmen, is evident as well from the general design as from the details. This is true, not only of the older part of the church, from the time of Archbishop Augustine (1161-1188), where the Anglo-Norman character of the work is so striking, but also as regards the later parts. Augustine maintained the closest connection with England, whither he repaired when compelled to fly from Norway; it was therefore to be expected both that he himself should send to that country for architects, and that his successors should follow his example."§ Probably the work is subsequent to the great fire of 1328 and

---

* See illustrations in *Gothic Architecture in England*, 478.

† This is seen also in the Ledbury window illustrated in *Gothic Architecture in England*, 474.

‡ At Great Bardfield the only modern part is the three statuettes, added about ten years ago. Stebbing screen is fourteenth-century work; an illustration of it before restoration appears in Buckler's *Essex Churches*, and in *Spring Gardens Sketch Book*, viii. 28.

§ Munch's *Trondhjem's Domkirke*, Christiania, 1859.

STONE SCREENS

Totnes

previous to the advent of the Black Death, the ravages of which were very great in Norway in 1350.

The fourth type is that of by far the largest number of parochial stone screens. It consists simply of reproductions of the design of wooden screens. A very beautiful example is that at Totnes, Devon (33), erected by the Corporation in 1459.* This screen was ordered to be made like that of the Lady Chapel at Exeter, but far exceeds it in beauty and elaborate detail. It is 60 feet long, and full of light tracery, rich with niches and tabernacle work. It is vaulted, like Tilbrook (111), on the

Colyton

west side only. All the tracery in the fan vaulting is pierced through.† Paignton, Devon, also has the remains of a very handsome stone screen. A pretty example is illustrated from Colyton, Devon (34).

Wherever there is a gabled wall at the east end of the nave, whether above a single or triple chancel arch, the broad expanse of plain masonry may be pierced by one or two apertures; by one, at Capel-le-Ferne (23), by two at Melton Constable,

* The Totnes screen is illustrated in the article "Screen" in the *Architectural Publication Society's Dictionary*.
† Mr Harry Hems in *Rood and Other Screens*, 11.

STONE SCREENS

Exeter Cathedral

Compton Bassett

Norfolk (7), Westwell (23), and Sandridge (28). What is the use of the hole or holes so high up? It is suggested that a tall ladder was set up in the chancel, and through the hole access was obtained to a rood loft. But why make two holes for that purpose? Besides, the apertures at Melton Constable are of Norman date, when no lofts as yet are known to have existed in parish churches. It might be that the rood was actually placed within the aperture, as nowadays it is at Capel-le-Ferne; unfortunately, where there are two holes, the explanation fails to hold water. Perhaps the object was that behind the rood there should not be whitewashed or frescoed wall, but the rood should be silhouetted against the darkness of the chancel.*

A very considerable number of chancel and parclose screens of stone are still to be found in our parish churches. They deserve, but have not yet received, a separate monograph.†

OAK v. STONE SCREENS

Some of the oak screens seem to have had for their predecessors screens of stone. In some cases there is a documentary evidence to that effect. At Tintinhull, Somerset, the churchwardens' accounts ‡ for 1451 describe the building of an oak rood loft, in which the lower part of an earlier stone screen was retained as foundation.

In some districts, *e.g.*, Devon, and much of Somerset and Wales generally, there was plenty of stone, but for the most part it was hard and intractable; while in East Anglia every scrap of freestone for windows, doorways, quoins, &c., had to be imported from quarries at far away Barnack or elsewhere. It is just in these districts (1) Devon and Somerset, (2) Norfolk and Suffolk, (3) the Welsh border, that by far the noblest wooden screens

---

* In Gothic days it was very common in the West of England, especially in Herefordshire, to insert a small window or a pair of small windows over the chancel arch. Later, a very big window occurs, *e.g.*, in Cirencester nave; illustrated in *Gothic Architecture in England*, 544. But these have nothing to do with lofts.

† In addition to those given above the following stone screens deserve mention:—Awliscombe and Poltimore, Devon; Bickenhill, Warwick; Brympton, Somerset; Broughton, Oxon.; Cerne Abbas, Dorset; Chelmorton and Ilkeston, Derbyshire; Croyland, Tattershall, and West Deeping, Lincolnshire; Darlington, Durham; Eastwell, Leicester; Charlton, Compton Bassett, Great Chalfield, Heytesbury, Highway, Hilmarton, Yatton Keynell, Wiltshire; Methley, Yorkshire; Nantwich, Cheshire.

‡ Edited by Bishop Hobhouse for the Somerset Record Society, 1890.

were erected, and the greatest number still remain. One cause of the unpopularity of the stone screen was that it did not develop in the right direction. In a parochial screen it was essential that it should be so open that the view of the high

Ottery St Mary

altar should be as little obstructed as possible. This was admirably secured in such triple window screens as those of Stebbing and Great Bardfield (29). But in these delightful compositions there was a fatal defect; they were not designed for a loft.*

* Till its restoration, the stone screen at Stebbing showed marks of having been cut for support to a wooden loft.

This type of screen being abandoned, the best course would have been to reproduce the Norfolk type of oak screen. Instead of that, it was the Devon type which usually was copied. In this type, each bay contains an unglazed window, crowded with mullions and tracery; but these, when executed in wood, could be cut into such slender and delicate form that the screen still remained comparatively open. Such delicate and fragile forms were difficult to copy in stone; if the stone mullions and tracery were made substantial, the screenwork was so massive as to impede the view, *e.g.*, at Colyton (34); if they were made delicate, the cost and fragility of the work were much increased. In the former, the East Anglian type, mullions and tracery are omitted, at any rate in the lower part of the opening. Such a type was well suited for reproduction in stone; but examples are scarce; they occur at Compton Bassett (35), and Paignton, Devon. There were indeed screens to which no such objection could be taken, *e.g.*, those at Bramford (24), and Bradford Abbas (26), which, while open below, provided supports for a loft and rood, but they were too few in number to influence the general run of design.

Walsoken

CONSTRUCTION OF OAK SCREENS

As far as is known, every wooden screen in the country, but one, is of oak. The one exception is at Rodmersham, Kent, where the screen has been pronounced by Mr Harry Hems to be of Spanish chestnut. Oak screens were of two parts; the upper part was constructed of open panels or of traceried panels, so that the high altar might be in view; the lower part was sometimes left more or less open, as at Walsoken, Norfolk (38); much more frequently it was of solid panels, either carved, or, in rich parishes, painted with figures of the saints and doctors of the Church. Occasionally, *e.g.*, at Bridford (138), tiny statuettes of saints are found in the lower panels. The sills upon which the rood screens stood were nearly always massive, and often very effectively moulded. As a rule, these sills run right through from end to end, under doors and under panelling alike; they must have been constant stumbling-blocks to successive generations when entering or leaving the chancel. Mr G. E. Street thus describes the general construction of screens:* "The lower panels of early screens were usually filled in with feather-edged, grooved and tongued boards. The 'monials,' or 'mullions,' were delicate columns; the tracery was very simple, and cut out of long pieces of board, from $2\frac{1}{2}$ to 4 inches thick. The capitals were pinned to the tracery with vertical oak pins, as at St John's, Winchester. In the later screens the lower part of the screen was panelled, the monials were moulded, and the whole work was much more complete." A similar account is given by Mr Harry Sirr.† "The usual framework of the screens," he says, "is quite simple. The principal uprights or 'muntins' are let into a stout oak sill upon the floor, from which they are carried to a strong upper beam some 15 feet above. On either side of this upper beam, somewhat higher up, another beam is let into the wall, or corbelled from it, forming the support for the loft; the intermediate space between each of these and the lower beam being filled in with bracketing for the support of the cornice, coving, or vaulting. Also, at some 4 feet from the floor, a cross rail is inserted, the space below, which is divided up by lesser muntins, constituting the framework for the lower panelling. This construction is increased or varied in the more elaborate examples. As regards the workmanship, the structural portion or framework is usually morticed and tenoned together, and pinned with oak pins. The finer and more delicate carved work, as also the tracery in the canopies of stalls, when joined, is jointed with a dowel, or occasionally a secret tenon here and there is left on the solid. Wherever the work admitted it, however, it was all got out of the solid; the tracery of the head of an entire compartment of a screen, for instance, being generally in one piece. At Yately, Hants, two traceried heads of the quire screen, each measuring 13 inches in depth, and 6 feet in length, are each out of one solid piece."

* Street's *Woodwork*, R.I.B.A. *Journal*, February 1865.
† *Art Journal*, 1883, p. 329.

Cost of Screens

Numerous entries are found in churchwardens' accounts as to payments for screens. The screen and loft at St Margaret's, Westminster, cost £38 besides £10 for rood and statues; total, £48; say £500 in our money. The screen at Ashburton, Devon, erected in 1525, cost £20. 1s. 6¼d.; say £200 in our money. At Crowcombe, Taunton, there was paid in the year 1729-30 to Mr Thomas Parker for making the screens, flooring, and wainscotting the altar, &c., £73. 10s. At Yatton, Somerset, the churchwardens' accounts for 1454 give the whole cost of the rood loft. The old loft cost 24d. to take down. The new work was done by J. Crosse, the village carpenter, who received £18. 13s., and again £3. 6s. 5d.; also 3d. for ale in setting up of the post of the rood loft; also 11s. 4d. for labour in the loft; also 2d. for ale given to Crosse at certain times in his work "to make him well-willed"; also £3. 10s. 7d. for images for the rood lofts. Also J. Smith was paid 23d. for charcoal used in iron work, and 13s. 4d. for the chandelier in the rood loft. Not including other items, such as glue, paint, gilding, &c., this rood loft cost over £27, or in our money £405.*

The indenture for the making of the rood loft at Old St Mary's, Cambridge,† remains. It was to extend across nave and aisles. "All the niches, crestings, groinings supporting the loft, panelling, flying buttresses, canopies, pinnacles, doors, gables, &c., to be of good substantial wainscot; the breast or western side of the loft to be copied from that in Tripplow Church, the eastern side from that in Gasseley Church. On the eastern side there was to be an eastern projection ('poulpete' or 'pulpit') into the midst of the choir. The loft to be 8 feet broad with such *yomags* ('images') as shall be advised and appointed by the parishioners, and all the yomags shall be of good pictures, forms, and vicenamyes ('physiognomies') without rifts, cracks, or other deformities. The uprights or standards to be of full seasoned oak." This work seems to have been finished in 1523, for in that year there was paid "viij*d*. for holowyng of ye Ymagesse of Mari and Jhon." Mr R. W. Goulding‡ has printed a very voluminous contract for making a rood loft, parclose screens, &c., at Stratton, Cornwall, in 1531, with John Dawe, of the parish of Lawhitton in Cornwall, and John Pares, of the parish of North Lew in Devon. There was to be a rood loft

---

* Hobhouse's *Churchwardens' Accounts of Yatton, &c.*
† *Publications of the Cambridge Antiquarian Society*, 1869, p. 64.
‡ *Records of Blanchminster's Charity*, Louth, 1898, p. 91.

right across the three "churches" ("naves") to be made after the pattern, form, and fashion as the rood loft of St Kew. Also a crucifix with a Mary and John after pattern, fashion, and workmanship as that in Liskeard Church. Also two altars of timber, of St Armell and the Visitation of our Blessed Lady, with tabernacles for the same at both ends of the said rood loft, one by the south wall, the other by the north wall of the church, wrought after the pattern and workmanship of St Kew. Also parclose screens on either side of the chancel, between the chancel and the chancel aisles. Also five seats or pews in the chancel aisles, three in the south aisle, and two in the north aisle. Also the old stalls were to be replaced. Also a loft was to be built above the north parclose screen to hold organs Also two dormer windows to be inserted in the nave roof above the crucifix like those at St Mary Weyke. Also the north aisle wall was to be made as lofty as that of the nave. Also a way to be made for the loft by or under the arches of the pier arcade. John Dawe and John Pares were to pay for the timber and its carriage, but not for the ironwork and masonry, and to keep everything in repair for four years after the completion of the work. They were allowed seven years for the work. The mode of payment was very curious. They were to be paid only for the rood loft across the church, and for that at the rate of 46s. 8d. per lineal foot, "for every foot of the breadth of the said Church of Stratton to be measured upon the ground along by the said rood loft." All the other work, the parcloses, seats, &c., to be thrown in. Up to the year 1539 payments had been made to the extent of £108, say £1,080 in our money. The indenture is interesting in many ways. The work was to be largely a copy of that in three other parish churches; similarly at Great St Mary, Cambridge, the screen in front was to be a copy of that at Tripplow, and at the back a copy of that at Gasseley; and the stone screen at Totnes was to be a copy of that of the Lady Chapel in Exeter Cathedral. Such copyism accounts at once for the great family resemblance of the screens in each district, *e.g.*, on the Welsh border, Devon, and East Anglia. A single man introduces a good design; it is copied in various directions; copies are made of copies; so grows up a distinct local school. In architecture also the same borrowing took place in the parish churches; and so the Somerset towers, the Kentish towers, the Sussex towers, the East Anglian towers, the Pembrokeshire towers, gradually developed into distinct schools. So it was with the wooden spires of South-eastern England, and the broach spires of Northamptonshire. So it was with the font, the porch, and every other member and accessory of the church. So, above all, it was with the plan; nothing can well be more like one another than the generality of plans in the churches of Cornwall, or more unlike those of the rest of England; the plan of Stratton is typical; the church consisting simply of three parallel naves, each with its own span roof. The whole country, owing to this system of borrowing, ultimately divided itself into well-defined architectural provinces.

Inscriptions

Here and there inscriptions are found. At Northenden, Cheshire, there is the inscription: "Have mercy on me, O Lord, according to Thy loving kindness; according unto the multitude of Thy tender mercies blot out my transgressions. Create in me a clean heart, O God, and renew a right spirit within me." A screen of 1691 at Probus, Cornwall, has the inscription: "Jesus, hear us, Thy people, and send us grace and good for ever." At Elworthy, Somerset, the screen has the inscription: "O Lord, prepare our arts to praye. Anno Domi, 1632." The following quatrain from Guilden Morden, Cambridge, is unexceptionable in piety, if not in prosody:—

> "Ad mortem duram Jhesu de me cape curam;
> Vitam venturam post mortem redde securam;
> Fac me confessum rogo Te Deus ante secessum,
> Et post decessum coelo michi dirige gressum."*

Atherington screen is pious and loyal in plain English: "God bless our church and Queen Elizabeth, and give us peace and truth in Christ. Amen." The Post-Restoration inscriptions breathe the soundest Toryism. At Milborne, Dorset, the inscription from Ecclesiastes runs: "Where the word of a king is, there is power, and none may say, What doest thou?" Soundly royalist also is the inscription on one side of the screen (1624) at Low Ham, Somerset: "My son, fear thou the Lord and the king, and meddle not with them that are given to change." On the other side is the inscription: "Christ is the end of the law for righteousness to every one that believeth." Beneath the Doom at Wenhaston (124) is a text which, from the lettering, appears to be of the time of Queen Elizabeth, and was probably added when the tympanum was whitewashed over. It runs as follows: "Let every soule Submyt him selfe unto the authorytye

---

* "In death's hard hour, Jesu, have care of me, and bring me safely to eternal life. Grant me to make confession ere I die, and when I die, direct my steps to heaven."

SCREEN DESIGN 43

Atherington

of the hygher powers for there is no power but of god The /
Powers that be are ordeyne^d of god but they that resest or are
againste the ordinaunce of god shall receyve to them selves
utter / damnacion For rulers are not fearefull to them that do
good but to them that do evyll for he is the mynister of god."
The text is taken from the Epistle of St Paul to the Romans,
xiii. 1-4.

44 SCREENS AND GALLERIES

Mobberley

SCREEN DESIGN

Mobberley

46   SCREENS AND GALLERIES

Southwold

SCREEN DESIGN 47

Southwold

Southwold

Screens of Norfolk and Suffolk, Devon and Somerset

Both in Norfolk and Suffolk, and in the south-west of England and Wales, the normal design of the great Gothic screens is in the main lithic. Take the range of clerestory windows and one-half of the lierne vault of Norwich quire, or the clerestory windows and half the fan vault of Sherborne, and you have the western or eastern side of such coved or vaulted screens as those of Mobberley, Cheshire (44), or High Ham, Somerset (65). The difference is that the screen is executed in wood, and that the windows are unglazed. On the whole, the western screens are much less lithic in design than those of East Anglia. In the latter the design is in the main architectural; there is often a profuse employment of tiny buttresses, pinnacles, string courses and hood-molds, and the battlement sometimes appears rather than open cresting. There is a distinctly different feeling in an eastern and a western cornice; the mouldings of the former are reminiscent of those of stone work; whereas a western cornice in its broad convex surfaces, separated by simple beads and little undercut, is reminiscent of the logs of which it is composed. It is, as it were, built up of logs piled horizontally one on the top of the other, prevented from slipping by the insertion of slender poles ("beads") between each pair of logs, *e.g.*, at Kenton (106), and Congresbury (64). So it is with the uprights or standards; even in rich examples they frankly acknowledge themselves to be but posts, *e.g.*, at Swymbridge (61) and Minehead (69). In the East Anglian screen, on the other hand, the cornice of the screen is more of a reproduction of the cornice of stone which crests the walls out of doors, forming the foundation of parapet or battlement. In the screen of Devon the feeling that it is a solid log construction is preserved throughout; it is solid, massive, and heavy, whereas an East Anglian screen is largely constructed in open work, and is light and airy; and, indeed, when looked at from a distance, the chancel screen, *e.g.*, at Southwold (46), Cawston (174), Worstead (50), is sometimes painfully thin, meagre, and wiry. The emphasis of massiveness and solidity comes out most forcibly in the cornice. In the western design the vast, heavy, black frowning cornice is the leading note; the windowed tracery down below is overshadowed into insignificance, however beautiful it may be, *e.g.*, at Bovey Tracey (62). And when the cornice is reinforced by a parapetted loft, the tracery of the openings does not even play a secondary part in the composition; *e.g.*, Staverton (108). But, in an East Anglian screen, the arch or the tracery plays the leading part; the cornice is comparatively insignificant, *e.g.*, the parclose screens of Southwold (47). It follows also that since the western cornice has the greater projection, below it there is a greater breadth of coving and vaulting, and there being larger scope for it, this is developed and enriched to a very great extent, *e.g.*, at Kenton and High Ham (65), as is well seen also in the fine screen of Astbury chancel,* Cheshire. Both in Devon and East Anglia very few screens have retained the parapets of their loft; in the former, however, a very large number of screens have retained the loft floor and the coving or vaulting beneath it. In East Anglia the destruction, as a rule, has been more sweeping; vaulting and coving and loft floor have perished together; the cornice has lost its projection altogether, and is flat with the tracery down below, *e.g.*, at Southwold (46), Lavenham (51), Hadleigh (52). A cornice without projection is a poor thing indeed, and the frequent survival of the loft floor with its supports in Devon and its rarity in East Anglia,† give one perhaps an unduly unfavourable impression of the design of the latter.

In estimating the value of East Anglian screen design, an important factor to be borne in mind is the position of the screen. The primary function of all screens is to serve as a barrier. But if it be a chancel screen, it ought to be a barrier of open character, so as to obstruct as little as possible the view by the congregation of the celebrant at the Mass. To this object no concession was made in Devon design. In East Anglia, however, a sharp distinction is often made between a screen in front of the high altar, and screens in any other position. The latter being mainly barriers, it is undesirable to have too much open work. Nowhere is this better seen than at Southwold, where the main screen (46) is of the lightest possible character, whereas the parclose screens are largely occupied by elaborate tracery. So also at East Harling (22), the screen, being that of the Lady Chapel, is constructed in the most massive fashion, and the mullions of the tracery are carried down to the middle rail, as if it were a screen of Devon. As regards the main screen across a chancel arch in Norfolk and Suffolk, the desire for openness was so strong that tracery was largely or wholly

* Measured drawing in *Architectural Association Sketch Book*, 3rd series, vol. 5.
† Loft floors, however, are shown at Southwold (47), Dennington (14), East Harling (22), in parclose screens; and at Worstead (50) and Bramfield (76), in quire screens.

Worstead from East

Lavenham

Hadleigh

SCREEN DESIGN

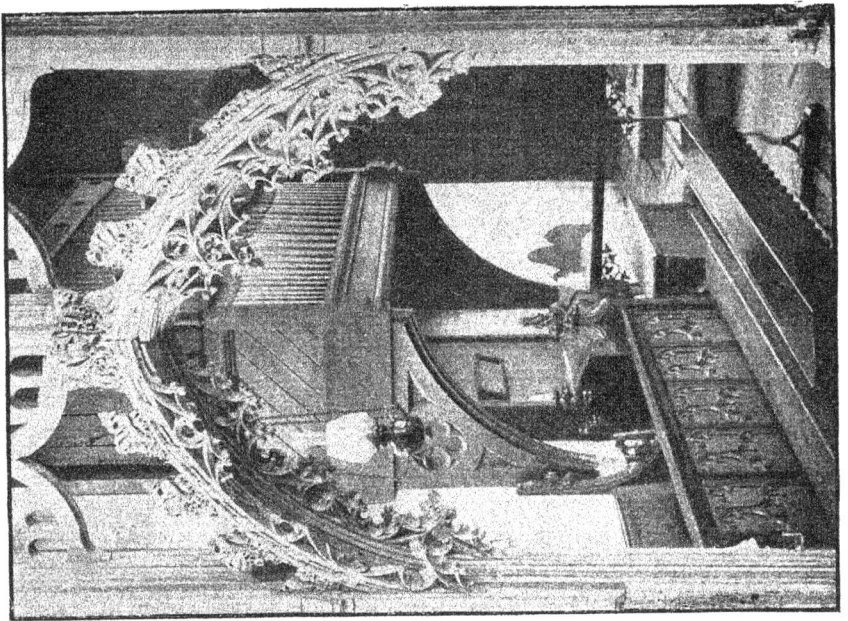

Yaxley

Barningham

sacrificed to secure it. Sometimes, as at Worstead (50), each arched panel has in its head a crocketed decorative arch; at Southwold (46) even this is omitted. In this, the most characteristic design of East Anglian chancel screen, the result is nowadays unsatisfactory, even at Worstead (1512), which is a favourable specimen, since it retains both its rood floor and groining,* and the subsidiary arches below. But before condemn-

Blundeston

Thurlton

ing it, we must in imagination replace the parapets of the loft. Then it is quite conceivable that a design concentrating itself on the loft and the great Rood, Mary and John above the loft, might be entirely adequate and satisfactory; perhaps even more than a western design, such as that of Staverton (108), in which, to some extent, the interest is dissipated by the calls made on the eye by the mullioned and traceried openings below. As things stand, it is perhaps not so much in the chancel screens of Norfolk

* The vaulting remains on the eastern side only.

SCREEN DESIGN

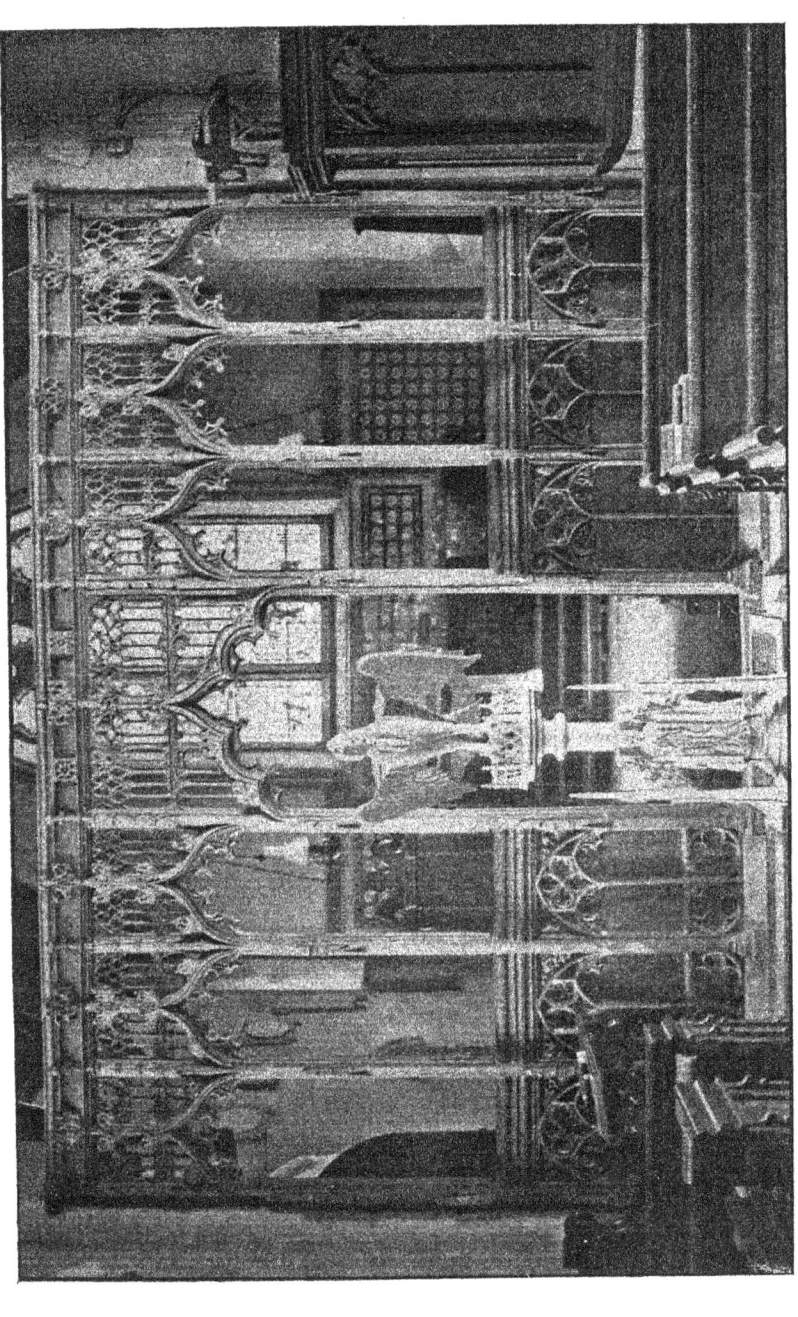

Scarning

and Suffolk as in the minor screens* that the most exquisite and consummate design is found. For decorative purposes the great favourite was a somewhat acutely pointed ogee arch, heavily crocketed, cusped, and finialled, of which good examples are seen at Blundeston (54), Worstead (50), Thurlton (54), Cawston (174), Acle (176), Barningham (53), Bramfield (76), Dennington (14). Sometimes the lower curve of the ogee emerges fully, as at East Harling (22); much more frequently, it is nearly or quite invisible. Above this ogee arch, and below the horizontal line of the cornice is a considerable space, which at Barningham and Dennington is charmingly filled with rectilinear tracery; less successfully at Blundeston and Thurlton, Suffolk.† But in the best designs a second arch is introduced close to the cornice; a pointed arch at East Harling, a stilted semicircular arch at Bramfield, a four-centred arch at Lavenham (19), delightful variety being obtained by the play of contrast in the arch below and the arch above. Or, as at Hadleigh (52), three tiers of pointed are contrasted with one tier of segmental arches; while in the Southwold parclose screen (47), segmental, semicircular, and ogee arches are played off one against another with delightful cleverness. Add to this the elaboration of the cusping; double and sometimes triple cusping occurs, *e.g.*, at Blundeston (54), and in the wonderful screen-doorways of the neighbouring churches of Eye and Yaxley (53), and one has architectural design of the very first order.‡ In execution also the eastern screens bear off the bell, as well as in versatility and ingenuity of design. It is true that in Devon there are a few screens, *e.g.*, Holbeton (frontispiece), of marked individuality, and that a few others, owing to foreign influence, have still greater distinction, *e.g.*, Colebrook (84), but on the whole, there is great similarity, almost monotony, of design as compared with the work of East Anglia.

In Devon, even in the best work, there is much less of

---

* Among minor screens we may include, for convenience, the chancel screens of such small churches as Barningham, Bramfield, Thurlton, and Blundeston.

† By exception the spandrels are left open in the chancel screen of Lavenham (51), a not wholly successful design.

‡ "On Ranworth screen and the pulpit of Burlingham are cast-lead ornaments gilded. At Ranworth each is at about 4-inch centres on the canopy ribs and round the main ornaments below the canopy and on the cornice of the posts at the projecting wings of the screen. The pattern of the ornament is a close imitation of a star-fish. At Worstead in the spandrels of the arches of the lower panels of the screen is a sort of lily ornament in cast lead. The lead ornaments at Ranworth and Burlingham are undoubtedly original, those at Worstead not so certainly so."—W. D.

SCREEN DESIGN

Walpole St Peter

II

58　　　　SCREENS AND GALLERIES

Hitchin, South Chapel

architectural design proper; the screens are magnificent, but they make their impression mainly by vastness of dimension, solidity, play of light and shade, and inconceivable richness of vegetative carving. Not that architectural design is absent. The tracery is very often indeed of the most exquisite beauty; it would be very difficult to produce any

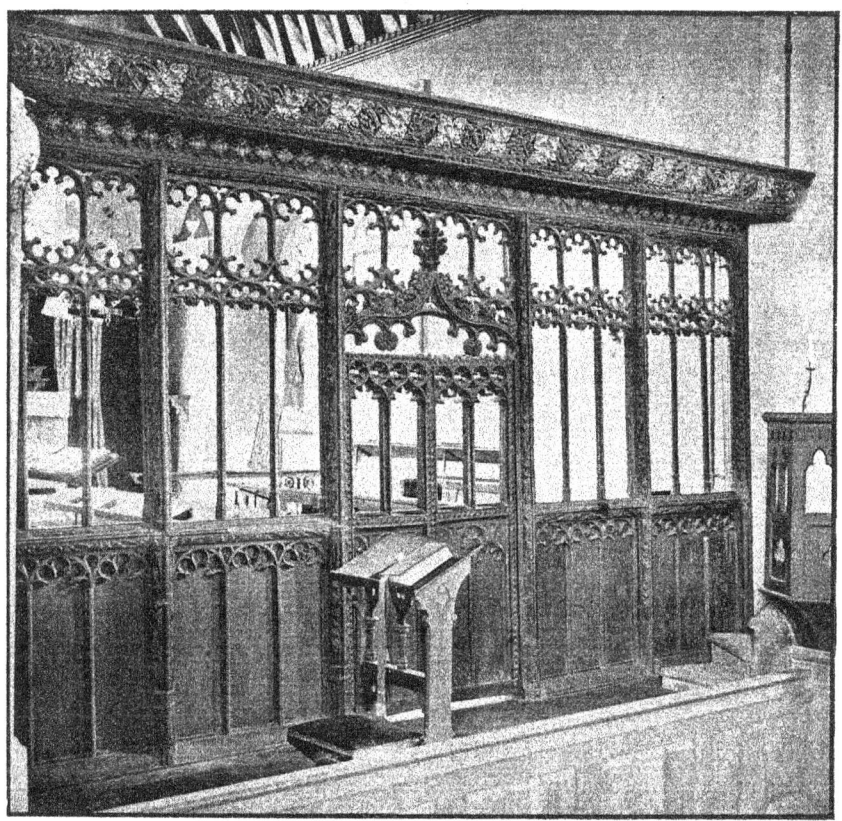

Stoke-in-Teignhead

in England, either in wood or stone, to surpass or even to equal that of Kenton, with its pretty contrast of pointed and ogee arches (106), or Holbeton, where an even higher level is reached by the superposition on stilted pointed arches of intersecting ogees (frontispiece). Very satisfactory, too, is the play of segmental and ogee arches against intersecting four-centred arches at Stoke-in-Teignhead (59); it might be in Norfolk, not in Devon.* In Somerset and Dorset, there is on the whole a falling off in tracery design ; nothing can indeed be more perfectly delightful than the tracery at Minehead (69); but the poetry of Minehead becomes very plain prose at Milborne Port (113), Somerset. In Devon the screens were full of design, crowded and exuberant with design from top to bottom. Below was panelling with paintings of saints, as at Kenton (106), and Staverton (108); † or, more rarely, with little figures in wood, as at Bridford (138). The standards were themselves often covered with delicate carving, as at Holbeton (frontispiece), and Bridford ; the mullions sometimes were channelled or clustered ; they had pretty moulded bases and capitals, and sometimes as at Holbeton, the capitals were reduplicated. No pains, no time, no cost was too excessive to be spent on the screen.

The cornices of the western screens are often truly magnificent. " At Congresbury, Somerset (64), the principal hollow of the cornice contains a wonderfully carved trailing vine, separated by beadings from a smaller enrichment above and below. The flowing or wavy branch of the vine is skilfully arranged to give as much strength as possible to the enrichment ; and it is so well managed, that from below one is unable to perceive that the wood is not actually pierced everywhere. The outline of each leaf is well emphasised by the piercings round it ; and within the piercings the entangled tendrils and the stem to the leaf are the only pieces of solid left, telling with matchless effect, holding the work well together, and connecting it throughout its entire length. Bunches of grapes above and below the leaves accommodate themselves to the horizontal enclosing line, and help to form a general plane to the convex section of the enrichment ; and together with the stem of the vine give thickness and solidity. The upper enrichment, of delicate workmanship, consists of a series of five-lobed flowers placed upright and reversed alternately. The lower enrichment consists of a small flower with a leaf on either side, is executed with sharp chiselling, and is rather bolder." ‡ In the cornice design the great joy was undulation of curve. The leaves themselves, *e.g.*, the great leaves at Bovey Tracey (63), are bulbous in the centre to produce alternation of ogee curve ; leaf flows on to leaf over tendrils, themselves undulating, as at High Ham (65) and Bovey Tracey ; or intertwined into tangles like "traveller's joy," as at Congres-

* This screen differs much from the normal screen of Devon, perhaps because of its early date, if it is correct, as stated, that it is of the time of Richard II.
† Both are "restorations."
‡ *Art Journal*, 1885, 148.

SCREEN DESIGN

Swymbridge

62 SCREENS AND GALLERIES

Bovey Tracey

SCREEN DESIGN

Bovey Tracey

64 SCREENS AND GALLERIES

SCREEN DESIGN

High Ham

bury and Bovey Tracey; at High Ham (65) they even curl round a twisted rope. The species of leaves employed are somewhat limited, and the leafage is duly conventionalised. Living observation and realistic reproduction of plant life and plant movement is confined to the tendrils; one must really be a botanist to realise the exact truth of the rendering of the various methods by which the creepers and climbers of the hedge-row secure and maintain their grip. In the rendering of detail the cornice work presents much similarity; it is not so with the composition as a whole. Quite a simple cornice is illustrated from Stoke-in-Teignhead (59). At Bovey Tracey (63), Bridford (138), and Holbeton (89), there are two principal members of about equal value; at Harberton (12) one member is large, the other small. At Kenton (106) there are three members, of which the central is small; at Dunchideock (118) the three members are of about equal importance; at Congresbury (64) the three are unequal in value. Even more elaborate cornices are found. We may fairly assume that the screen at High Ham, Somerset, represents the high-water mark of the art of the day; for it was erected in 1476 at the cost of Abbot Selwood of Glastonbury, aided by Lord Poulett and the rector of the church, John Dyer. With such resources, elaboration of design was to be expected, and the cornice (65) contains no less than five bands of carved ornament, separated by single, double, or triple beads.

Yet further to add to the beauty of the cornice, and somewhat to lighten its massive solidity, it was given a cresting of open work, sometimes at the top only, as at High Ham (65), but often, reversed, at the bottom also, as at Kenton (106), Dunchideock (118), and Swymbridge (61). What exquisite design informed these crestings, a glance will show at High Ham, Holbeton (89), and Atherington (67). Very frequently the cresting has been broken, as at Low Ham, perhaps when the loft and organs were removed; and was then often removed altogether. Above the cornice again came a magnificent parapet, with its own cornice and cresting, *e.g.*, at Atherington, where some of it remains *in situ*. How magnificent was the general effect of a screen with rood loft complete is well seen at Kenton (106), Lew Trenchard, Staverton (108), and elsewhere, where the lofts have recently been replaced. The eastern front of the loft was divided into a series of narrow panels, each containing the painting of a saint, sheltered by the most exquisite open work tabernacles imaginable.* Such are these wonderful memorials of the mediæval

* In the Atherington example the paintings of the frieze have been defaced, and a bar on the left cut away to make room for a later shield (43).

Marwood

art of England, which to the ignorance and indifference of the twentieth-century Englishman are as though they had never been.

And who did this western work? It is often assumed that, even if foreigners had not to be called in to do our woodwork, at any rate the best of it was executed at important centres such as London and Exeter; or, in default of that, that it was executed by gangs of peripatetic craftsmen. The simple truth, says Bishop Hobhouse, seems to be that in Devon and Somerset most of the work was done by the villagers themselves. Knowing the achievements of the British workman nowadays, it certainly seems inconceivable that the once grand chancel screen at Yatton, Somerset, for which, c. 1454, the carpenter's account alone amounted to £27, say £405 of our money, was executed on the spot by J. Crosse, who lived at Cleeve, within the parish; the oak being bought by the churchwardens in standing trees, which they selected, felled, and seasoned.* But in those days the craftsman was an artist, the artist a craftsman. Even now Devon is crowded with good things. No less than one hundred and fifty screens still remain in Devon, more or less perfect. Great numbers, however, have been destroyed. Mr F. Bligh Bond† gives a list of seventy-two screens which are known to have been destroyed in the nineteenth century by the clergy, their guardians. Mr Harry Hems gives many sad details.‡

So very numerous and fine are the screens in Norfolk and Suffolk, that it is hardly possible to draw up a list of pre-eminent examples, especially as the best design is often found in minor screens. In Norfolk—Edingthorpe, the Burlinghams, Trunch; St John Timberhill, Norwich; Sheringham, among very many others, are interesting; for painted panels the best perhaps are Ranworth, Barton Turf, Cawston, Marsham, Ludham, North Walsham, Aylsham, Strumpshaw. Ranworth is placed first both by Mr G. E. Fox and by Mr W. Davidson. "The infinite variety of ornament at Ranworth," says the latter, "the harmonious spacing, the clever invention, are unsurpassed. It is true that here and there the craftsmen have got a little bit out of scale with the section of a moulding or an ornament; but, taking architectural and decorative art combined, it is unquestionably the finest screen in East Anglia. Marsham has finer and more

---

* Hobhouse's *Somerset Records*, 4, xx. The fine bench ends also at Tintinhull in the same county were made in the parish, "33s. 3d. being paid in 1511 to the carpenter for sawing of timber for seats for the church, and for cutting and framing part of the same"; in the following year, 41s. 1d. were spent on seats.

† *Devonshire Screens*, 549, 550.

‡ *On Rood and other Screens*, pp. 2-11.

Minehead

delicately painted floral ornament; Cawston has a finer sense of proportion in the section of the mouldings, and more character—almost too much character—in some of the heads of the saints, *e.g.*, St Philip and St Matthias (74). Barton Turf has more spirituality of feeling in the figures, and is probably finer in the technique of its painting; but the uniqueness of the Ranworth design, with its parcloses and double-vaulted canopy, amply compensates for these deficiencies."* In Suffolk also there is a great wealth of fine screens, *e.g.*, Southwold, Lavenham, Sudbury, Parham, Bramfield, Eye, Barningham, Dennington. In Devon, among the very numerous fine examples may be mentioned the stone screens of Totnes, Paignton, Ottery St Mary, Colyton; and the oak screens of Abbot's Kerswell, Alphington, Ashton, Atherington, Aveton, Berry Pomeroy, Bovey Tracey, Bradninch, Bridford, Broadhempstone, Broadwoodwidger, Brushford, Burrington, Chawleigh, Chumleigh, Clyst St Lawrence, Colebrook, Coleridge, Cruwys Morchard, Cullompton, Combe Martin, Dartmouth, Dunchideock, Feniton, Harberton, Hartland, Holbeton, Holne, Honiton, Ilsington, Ipplepen, Kentisbere, Kenton, Lapford, Lew Trenchard, Littleham, near Bideford (copied from Patricio), Manaton, Marwood, Monkleigh, North Molton, Ottery St Mary, Peyhembury, Pilton, Plymstock, Plymtree St John, Rattery, Staverton, Stoke-in-Teignhead, Stokenham, Swymbridge, Tawstock, Tor Brian, Uffculme, Washfield (1624), Willand, Wolborough. In Somerset also good screenwork is very abundant, *e.g.*, Brimpton (stone), Banwell, Bicknoller, Brushford, Queen Camel, Carhampton, Congresbury, Croscombe, Crowcombe, Dunster, Fitzhead, High Ham, Low Ham, Milborne Port, Minehead, Norton Fitzwarren, Pilton, Raddington, Timberscombe, Trent, Trull, Withycombe.†

PAINTED SCREENS

In painted screens, Norfolk and Suffolk have an unquestionable superiority, for, whereas their paintings are refined works of

* "There are references to various Norfolk screens in the *Proceedings of the Norfolk and Norwich Arch. Soc.* as follows :—i. 324; ii. 280; iii. 18, 19, 69; iv. 298, 301, 345; vi. 306; vii. 182, 211; viii. 35, 337; ix. 369. In the *Eastern Counties Collectanea*, 1872-3, particulars respecting screens are to be found on pp. 61, 81, 95, 96, 97, 125, 126, 133, 143, 151, 154, 185, and 226."—W. T. B.

† Extended lists of screens, arranged by counties, are given in *English Church Furniture*, 102-143. For illustrations of the screens at Cullompton and Littleham, South Devon, see *Exeter Diocesan Society's Journal*, i. 3, v. 9; for that of Long Aston, Somerset, see Bowman, *Gothic Architecture*, viii.

Ranworth—St George

Ranworth—St Michael

art,* those of Devon and Somerset are mostly "of rude and conventional design and coarse in execution, though they are picturesque in their ugliness, and very valuable archæologically, and for their symbolism" "Nothing can exceed the richness of detail in the painted ornamentation of the eastern screens. The delicate flower and spray work which fills every hollow of the mouldings and is powdered over the backgrounds of the figures, the wonderful elaboration of the patterns of the dresses, the delicately applied gilding, all combine to make up a whole of the greatest beauty. And to enhance the effect on some of the larger and later screens the backgrounds of the pictures are worked in gesso in the most delicate relief and richly gilt. Even the broad flat fillets of the mullions are covered with gesso, stamped in intricate patterns of tracery, and having at intervals diminutive niches with tiny figures painted in them, which are protected by morsels of glass set in the pattern as in a frame. For splendour of effect and for multiplicity of forms in the gesso work, certainly none can surpass that at Southwold, Suffolk."† Of Italian influence in the painting of the Norfolk screens there is but little evidence. A more likely source would be the Netherlands, but in the fourteenth, fifteenth, and sixteenth century not a single Flemish name occurs. "On the other hand many of the names are distinctly English, being those of villages in Norfolk and Suffolk, *e.g.*, Frenze, Bradwell, Castleacre, Ocle or Acle, Hickling." Moreover, municipal and other registers record the names of quite a large number of painters who were permanent residents in Norwich between 1373 and 1579.‡ It is pointed out, however, by Mr E. F. Strange that on the Ranworth screen is a panel picture of the Temptation of St Anthony by Rufus van Dycken, who was in Antwerp in 1509 when he published this engraving; the furniture depicted in the room is Flemish, and the treatment is in every way the same.

The use of gesso was very common, *e.g.*, at Aylsham, Bur-

* They should be compared with the masterly painted panel in Norwich Cathedral described by Mr W. H. St John Hope in *Norfolk Arch. Soc. Journal*, xiii. 293.

† Mr G. E. Fox in *Arch. Journal*, xlvii. 66, and in *Victoria History of Norfolk*, ii. 547. For the processes employed in the painting and gesso work of the Norfolk screens see page 549. As the Southwold screens do not fit their position, Mr Davidson is of opinion that they were brought from some other church or churches. Many churches in the neighbourhood have perished, *e.g.*, several in the once great port of Dunwich; of Walberswick only the tower and an aisle remain. The vast church of Covehithe is roofless, and inside its great nave a little thatched chapel amply suffices for the remaining parishioners. All the above churches doubtless had formerly magnificent screens.

‡ For list see *Vict. Hist. of Norfolk*, ii. 552.

K

Cawston—St Philip   St Matthias

lingham, St Andrew, and Worstead; the substance is always gilded over when applied to screen work and panel paintings. Figures painted on vellum or on paper and glued over older work are found on the panels of some Norfolk screens of the sixteenth century, *e.g.*, at Cawston and Gateley.

The lower panels of the East Anglian screens are invariably solid and generally are painted. When so decorated each pair of panels was red or green, or each panel alternately. Our ancestors were remarkably fond of green; Mr André only noticed one exception, Gillingham, where blue and red are the colours employed. To this day the districts where the finest painted screens are found—Ranworth, Barton Turf, Ludham, Marsham — where the soil is dry, are incarnadine with poppies; where it is marshy, with lush green grass. The colour system of the screens is just that of Poppyland and Marshland blended.* On these red or green grounds were either angels, saints, and prophets, or simply floral patterns or powderings.† Occasionally the crowned initial of a saint formed the pattern, as at Salhouse, where the mitred N stands for the patron saint of the church, St Nicholas.‡ At Bramfield, Suffolk (76), the panels of the groining are painted blue and studded with gold. The ribs are white with margins of red, and green and purple flowers with gold blossoms are painted on the white. All the most prominent moldings of the traceried heads are gilt, while the undercut hollows are coloured red. The blue used is intensely deep; the red very rich, slightly approaching chocolate; and the green is dark, of a slightly brownish or red hue. There is a great variety in the painted ornamental forms, which on the fillets of the uprights take the shape of flowers with elegantly curved stems; on the ogee moldings broad pieces of flowers in green and brown alternately, with gilt centres, cover up portions of the white ground, and give a wavy look. On the blue moldings white fleurs-de-lis are painted. A description can but give a faint idea of the splendour and richness of the work, the effect of which is much enhanced by the elaborate stampings in mastic, covered with gilding, on the face of the main fillets.§

* " The red of the poppy, the gold of the corn, the yellow, blue, and green of the flowers on the screens, and in many cases the designs of the diapers, are taken from local plants, insects, and natural objects, conventionalised however to qualify them for their decorative position."—W. D.

† " In many cases where blue has been used it has faded, leaving the plain oak. The painters no doubt discovered this and used it sparingly." W. D.

‡ A beautiful series of devices from the Norfolk and Suffolk screens will be found in Pugin's work on *Floral Ornament*.

§ *Art Journal*, 1885, 148.

Bramfield

Everywhere in these Norfolk screens is seen the individual touch of the craftsman. There is nothing of uniformity, and consequently nothing of monotony. "At Ranworth," says Mr Davidson, "the apparent reckless spacing of the diapers and rosettes is most astonishing. Nearly everything seems to have been spaced by the eye; if a stencil was used, the patterns must afterwards have been touched up by hand. Mouldings, which if run by a machine would have been uniform, are in some cases double the size. . . . So also at Cawston no two of the diapers of the background are alike. The ornament varies so much that it is certain that most of the spacing and dividing must have been done by unaided hand and eye; the wave-pattern varies as much as from $1\frac{1}{2}$ to $3\frac{1}{2}$ inch centres."

Welsh Screens

In Wales screens are found chiefly on or near the Welsh border, viz., in Denbigh, Montgomery, Radnor, and Brecon · they are also common in the adjoining portions of Shropshire, Hereford, and Monmouth. These little out-of-the-way churches,* such as Peterchurch and Patricio, have retained much of their mediæval equipment and well repay the visit of the ecclesiologist. It may be that in some the Welsh-speaking parishioners did not understand, perhaps did not try to understand, the stream of royal proclamations which rained down on the parishes of England and Wales in the first half-century after the Reformation. Nor, perhaps, would the Commissioners be very anxious to visit in person these inaccessible mountain hamlets to see that royal injunctions had been carried out. These Welsh screens are of very considerable interest, partly because, occurring in such out-of-the-way little churches, they must be village work; partly because they have preserved so many lofts and tympana. Artistically, they are connected, as was to be expected, not with distant East Anglia, but with Devon and Somerset. As in that architectural province, the lofts are very broad, and have black-shadowed cornices of great projection, as at Llanrwst (83); and, where the parish could afford it, they have elaborate coving or

* Fine screens remain at Llanrwst and Derwen, Denbigh; Montgomery and Llanwnog, Montgomery; Llananno, Radnor; Llangwm, Monmouth; Llanegryn, Merioneth; Patricio, Brecknock. For the screens at Newport, Llanwnog, and Llananno see illustrated articles in the *Montgo1ery Collections*, vols. iii., iv., and vii. There are measured drawings of Llanegryn in the *Architect1ral Association Sketch Booh*, 2, viii. 19; of Derwen in the *Spring Gardens Sketch Booh*, ii. 50; of Patricio in ditto; of Llanrwst in the *Architect1ral Association Sketch Booh*, 1, xi. 1.

SCREENS AND GALLERIES

Patricio

Patricio

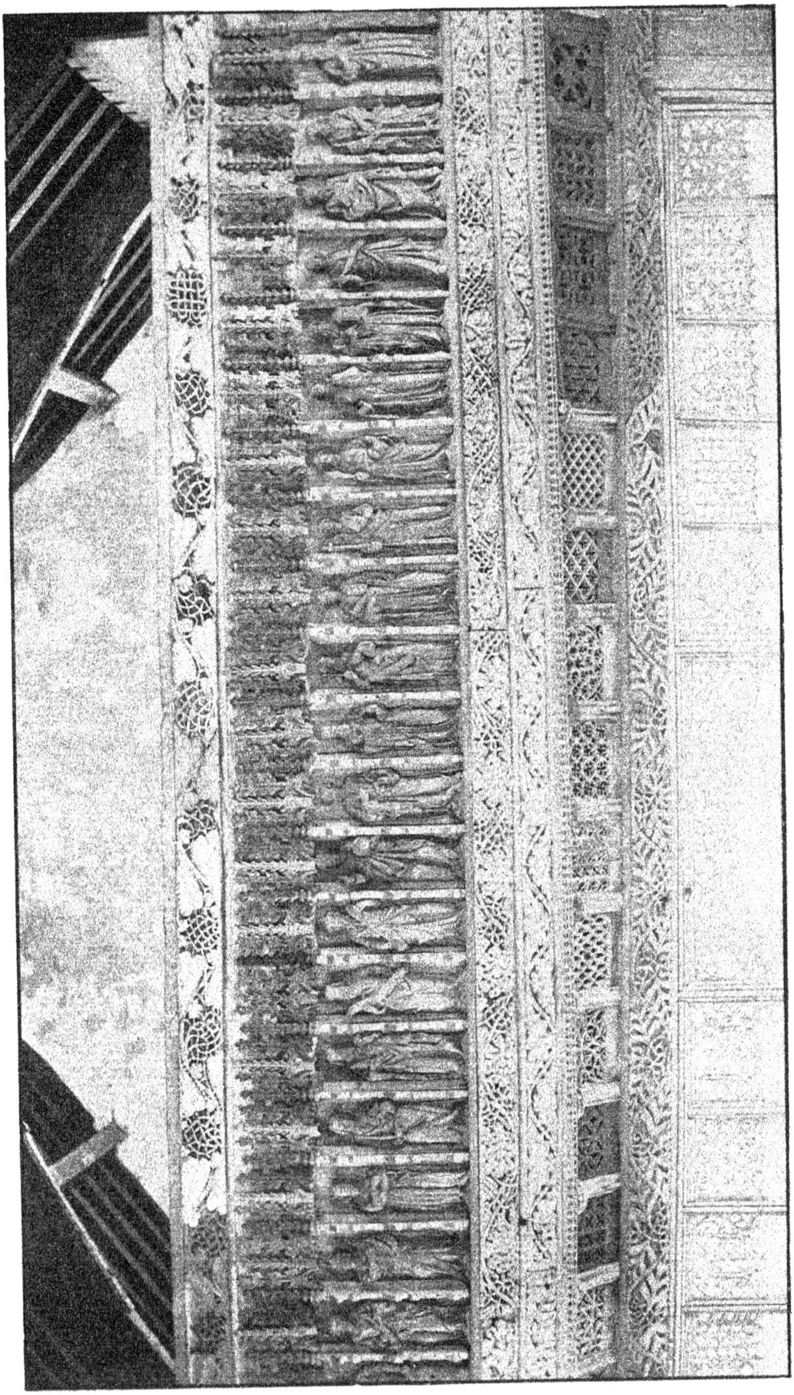

80 SCREENS AND GALLERIES

Llananno

Llananno

Llanrwst

Llanrwst

84　　　　　　SCREENS AND GALLERIES

Coe brook

St Fiacre-le-Faouet

groining, as again at Llanrwst; at Llananno (81) this is reduced to decorative panelling; at Patricio (78) and St Margaret's, Herefordshire (112), the loft supports are still simpler in character. The undulatory tendril work of the cornices of Llananno, Llanrwst, Patricio, Bettws Newydd (179), and Llanegryn (178) would find themselves at home anywhere in Devon. Equally akin to the eastern parapets of Atherington (43), Kenton (106), Staverton (108), are those of Llanrwst and Llananno, with their wealth of tabernacled canopies, small and great.* But there are Welsh peculiarities as well. One is the decoration with filigree work of the western parapets of the lofts of Patricio (79), Llanegryn (178), and Bettws Newydd (179), and of the eastern parapet of Llanrwst (83).† Another is the acceptance of non-lithic design. Llanrwst, indeed, has window openings in the screen, but the others illustrated have simply post and lintel construction; it is true that the window openings in these latter have tracery, nevertheless the openings themselves are square-headed. Nothing can be more frankly post and lintel construction than the screens of Bettws, Llanegryn, and Patricio. Add to this the fondness for arches straight-sided or nearly so—again, and very properly, a non-lithic design—in doorways, *e.g.*, at Llananno (81), and beneath the cornice of the screen, *e.g.*, at Llanrwst (82), and the small filigree character of the tracery everywhere, and it will be seen that the Welsh screens have quite a physiognomy of their own.

These then are the three main architectural provinces of screen design: that of Norfolk and Suffolk, that of Devon and Somerset, and that of the Welsh Border. But interesting examples of screen work occur all over the country, whose genealogical connection is still to determine.‡

Foreign Screens

Our screen design in general, especially that of late screens with rectilinear tracery, is so thoroughly English that in

---

* The two minor canopies shown at Llanrwst (82) originally extended right across the eastern front of the loft.

† These perforated panels appear in the loft parapet of the far away church of Hubberholme, Yorkshire.

‡ Mr Aymer Vallance has characterised the screens of Kent and Derbyshire in *Memorials of Old Kent* and *Memorials of Old Derbyshire*. Dr E. Mansel Sympson has described the Lincolnshire screens in the *Associated Societies Reports*, xx. 185. Those of Montgomery are described by Archdeacon Thomas in *Archæologia Cambrensis*, 6, iii. 96; those of Devon and Somerset by Mr F. Bligh Bond.

the vast bulk of it no suspicion of foreign influence can be admitted. There are, however, some few screens which are decidedly of foreign and not of English design. The screenwork at Colebrook* (84), Coleridge, and Brushford, Devon, is almost a facsimile of the peculiar Flamboyant of Brittany, *e.g.*, St Fiacre-le-Faouet (85). For this work Breton workmen must have been brought over to Devon. The screenwork in Carlisle Cathedral attributed to Prior Gondibour (1484-1507)† is of French Flamboyant character. That of Prior Salkeld (1542-1547), and that at Cartmel (90), are plainly the work of hands trained in the work of the early French Renaissance. The screenwork at Kenton, Devon (106), has been, rather unnecessarily, supposed to show Flemish influence. The design of the screen at Holbeton, Devon (89), has been attributed to Spanish influence; but it is a long cry from Spain to Devon, and of all the folk in England those of Devon hated Spaniards most. Moreover, the design of the tracery consists of intersecting four-centred arches, a thoroughly English motif.‡

CHRONOLOGY OF SCREENS

Of parochial screenwork none is earlier than the thirteenth century. The nearest approach to Norman screenwork in a parish church is to be seen at Compton, Surrey. This is a tripartite church, with unvaulted nave and quire, and a low vaulted sanctuary. Above the vault of the latter is a chapel, which is protected to the west by a wooden balustrade of late Norman design. But this is not a screen; it is put there simply to prevent people in the chapel from falling over on to the pavement of the quire.

In the thirteenth century also examples are rare. All that can be enumerated are one at Kirkstead, Lincolnshire; another now at the west end of Thurcaston Church, Leicester; some fragments at Benniworth, Lincolnshire; the screen at Stanton Harcourt, Oxon.§ (168), which retains its original hinges, lock, and bolt; and perhaps screens at Llandinabo and Pixley, Hereford. In France there are no screens of any sort earlier than the thirteenth century.

* Illustrated in *Spring Gardens Sketch Book*, viii. 34. For Coleridge see *Exeter Diocesan Society*, 1, i. 5.
† Illustrated in Billings' *Carlisle Cathedral*.
‡ "Lullington, Kent, is absolutely Flemish."—A. V.
§ Measured drawings of Kirkstead in *Spring Gardens Sketch Book*, viii. 8, and of Stanton Harcourt in *Spring Gardens Sketch Book*, ii. 2.

Kenton

RENAISSANCE DETAIL

Holbeton

Cartmel

Cartmel

King's College, Cambridge

Sparsholt

Fritton

In the fourteenth century an early example remains at Northfleet, Kent. But between 1315 and the advent of the Black Death, screen-building set in vigorously in many districts; many charming simple screens survive in East Anglia and elsewhere, *e.g.*, Fritton, Suffolk (92); Watlington, Norfolk (172), and Santon Downham, Suffolk (93).* It is remarkable that in Devon hardly a scrap of woodwork of any kind occurs before the fifteenth century. Mr Street thought that it had existed, but had been swept away by the carvers of the fifteenth and sixteenth century. There could, however, have been very little of it, or fragments

Santon Downham

would certainly survive. It was not till the end of the century, or later, that the great screen-building period set in generally. In many cases it was the last piece of work done before the Reformation. It often happened, especially in East Anglia, that the whole church had been rebuilt, the chancel late in the fourteenth, the nave in the fifteenth century; it had been provided with a superb tie-beam, arch-braced, or hammerbeam roof;

* Other fine examples remain at St Mary's Hospital, Chichester; St Margaret's, Lynn; Edingthorpe, Norfolk; Broughton, Oxon.; Guilden Morden, Cambridge; Long Itchington, Warwick; North Crawley, Bucks; Merton, Norfolk; Southacre, Norfolk (measured drawings in *Spring Gardens Sketch Book*, iii. 67).

a new porch and parvise of knapped flints had been built; every window had been filled with stained glass; a great soaring screen, loft, and rood consummated the work. In Norfolk, Mr G. E. Fox states that the dates of such screens with painted panels as can be ascertained with reasonable certainty range from 1451 to 1528.* In Kent, Mr Aymer Vallance has ascertained that the screens range from 1413 to 1521. Mr F. Bligh Bond is of opinion that few of the Devonshire screens can have been erected before 1420 or 1430, and that the most characteristic were probably erected about half a century later.†

Even in the fifteenth and sixteenth century the screen-building movement was sporadic, just as was the church-rebuilding movement. Both were commonest in those parts of England where there was peace and prosperity, great tracts of England where the Wars of the Roses hardly penetrated;‡ where the staple was wool, where the farmer was rich because of the high price of wool, where the weaver and merchant were rich with weaving and trading in wool, and where people thought nothing too good for their religion and their church.

Many of the screens of the first part of the sixteenth century are particularly interesting, for they illustrate charmingly the battle between the Romanticists and the Classicists, Gothic and Renaissance. They naturally fall into two classes: those which are purely Gothic still, a very large class, and those which have a delightful intermixture of Gothic and Renaissance. In the latter, just as in the chantry tombs of the Countess of Salisbury at Christchurch and of the Delawarrs at Broadwater and Boxgrove, and the chantry chapel of Bishop West at Ely, the whole of the constructional members retain Gothic forms; it is only in the minor detail that classical ornament appears. As is well known, the Early Renaissance movement in England was entirely due to Italian artists who came over at the request of Henry VIII., Cardinal Wolsey, Lord Marney, and other travelled members of the Court, and their work is practically confined to the South of England. Some of them certainly reached Devonshire, for there

---

* "The screen at South Walsingham bears the date 1538."—W. D.

† Measured drawings in the *Spring Gardens Sketch Book* of Acle screen, viii. 14; Cawston screen, vii. 3 to 6; Totnes screen, ii. 38; Ludham screen, iv. 68; Addlethorpe screen, vi. 51; Hawton, Notts, v. 43 and 44; Luton, Beds, v. 56 and 57; and in the *Architectural Association Sketch Book* of Cliffe screen, Kent, 2, i. 16.

‡ To read the superficial *Histories of England* one would imagine that all the villages in England were campaigning for many generations; whereas, even at Bosworth Field, the turning point in the warfare, Richard III. probably had no more than 5,000 men, and the Lancastrians about as many more.

Croscombe

96 SCREENS AND GALLERIES

Washfield

Washfield

Yarnton

Stonegrave

are found numerous screens with indubitable Italian ornament.*
Of these the earliest is the screen at Bridford, Devon, containing,
however, little Renaissance detail. It is said to be of 1508, but
that is an impossibly early date; twenty years later would be
early enough (138). An interesting group of these Gothic-
Renaissance screens occurs in the churches of Brancepeth
(1626-1633), Sedgefield, Merrington, and Ryton (1617-1630), in

St Paul's, Warden

the county of Durham. The screen at Low Ham, Somerset, is
an interesting specimen of Caroline Gothic.

For a short time after the Reformation few screens were built,
but by the beginning of the seventeenth century the Reformed

* Mr F. Bligh Bond instances the screens at Swymbridge, Lapford,
Atherington, Morchard Bishop, Poltimore, Bridford, Lustleigh, Marwood,
and South Pool.

Church seemed to be fairly consolidated, and screen building went on again merrily—now, however, and henceforth, almost always without lofts, and never with roods. Some of these screens have survived the hostility of the Gothic "revivalist" to all that savours of classical art. Very many, however, have been destroyed at "restorations," *e.g.*, the fine screen of Wimborne Minster (1610); Sir Gilbert Scott destroyed the Jacobean work of the Cirencester screen, and in Durham Cathedral the massive screen presented by that good Churchman, Bishop Cosin, who also had put up the Brancepeth screen and stalls; some fragments of the Durham screen may be found here and there in Durham Castle. The churches of Croscombe, Somerset (1616), (95), and St John's, Leeds (1634), are treasure houses of Jacobean woodwork; in the latter the screen extends right across the church. Grandest of all are the stalls and screen of Cartmel (90) and of King's College, Cambridge (91). It is hardly conceivable that any Englishman should have designed such exquisite work at so early date—work comparable with the best examples of Early Renaissance art in Italy or France. The screen at King's College has on it, several times repeated, the initials of Anna Regina and Henricus Rex, which fixes its date to the time when Anne Boleyn was queen, 1532-1536. To the same period belong the lower parts of the stalls; the coats of arms were given in 1633, and the canopies above the stalls in 1675-1678.*

It was not till Hanoverian days that screen building died away. Eighteenth-century screens are rare. Screens were put up early in the eighteenth century at Harlow and Great Dunmow, Essex. At Crowcombe, Somerset, the chancel received a lofty and handsome screen in 1729-30. One of the finest screens and parcloses in England, however, of purely classical type, is that at Cruwys Morchard, Devon (1814); it consists of an arcade of graceful Corinthian columns, carrying architrave, frieze, and cornice, while above the doorway of the screen is a classical pediment. That at St Paul's, Warden (98), is an interesting classical design.

* Other good examples are Tilney All Saints', Norfolk (1618), (sketch by Sir Charles Nicholson in *Architectural Association Sketch Book*, 3, i. 55); Holdenby and Passenham, Northants (1623); Trentham, Stafford; Rodney Stoke (1625), (109), Somerset; St Peter's, Cornhill, and the screen of All Hallows, Thames St., removed to St Margaret's, Lothbury, London; Stonegrave, Yorkshire (97); Countisbury and Washfield (1624), Devon (96), North Baddesley (1608), and Empshott (1624), Hants; Dore (1634), and Monington, Hereford; and Staindrop, Durham.

100   SCREENS AND GALLERIES

The Rood

The rood went by various names. Sometimes it is styled the great rood, or the high rood, or the good rood; sometimes the great cross, the high cross, or the greatest cross; sometimes the great crucifix, or the high crucifix. It was usually framed of timber, richly carved, painted, and gilt. The Blessed Virgin and St John were the accompaniment of the crucifix, but cherubim were occasionally added; there are rare instances where the four Evangelists were substituted for St Mary and St John.* The injunctions against further use of roods were exceptionally stringent, and the destruction was very thoroughgoing. An example is said to survive at Bettys-Gwerfil-Goch, near Corwen, Wales. The three figures are rudely carved on a panel in low relief, which was formerly affixed on or in front of the rood loft; it now forms the reredos over the communion table. On one side is a Mary, in a veiled headdress, a nimbus over the head, and the hands folded on the breast; on the other is a John, holding his right hand to his head; in one outer compartment are the pincers, thorns, and nails; in the other a hammer, the reed with the hyssop, and a spear; it is all rude work of the fifteenth century. Fragments of another rood remain at Mochre, Montgomery.† Dineley in *An Account of the Progress of His Grace Henry, the First Duke of Beaufort, through Wales, 1684*, mentions having seen in Llanrwst Church the wooden image of the crucifix belonging to the rood loft there. "Over the Timber Arch of the Chancell, near the Rood Loft, lieth hid the ancient figure of the Crucifixion as bigg as the life. This, I suppose, is shewn to none but the curious."

The position of the rood varied. The most effective position must have been beneath a lofty chancel arch, where the three figures would be silhouetted against the receding perspective of the quire. When, however, the chancel arch was low, the rood would have for background merely the masonry above the arch. In such a situation it would lose much of its effectiveness. This could be remedied by constructing a supplementary arch or arches above the main chancel arch, as was occasionally done, *e.g.*, at Melton Constable, Norfolk (7), and at Capel-le-Ferne, Kent (23); in the latter there is an arch of 6 feet by $5\frac{1}{2}$ feet behind the rood.

Just as the altar was shrouded from view by the Lenten veil

---

* In the screen of St Fiacre-le-Faouet (85), Brittany, on either side of the rood are shown, not Mary and John, but the two thieves.

† They are described and illustrated in *Archæologia Cambrensis*, iii. 96.

Broadwater

Charlton-on-Otmoor

from the first Sunday in Lent to the Thursday in Holy Week, so over the images of the rood veils were tightly drawn during the Lenten weeks. Cloths of red silk and crimson velvet are mentioned in the inventories as belonging to roods, and may have been used for this purpose. And just as it was customary to veil the rood and the Mary and John at penitential seasons, so it was usual at festivals to dress them with nosegays and garlands, and to decorate the loft with branches of trees. At Charlton-on-Otmoor, Oxon. (102), the practice of dressing a cross is still kept up. The accounts of St Peter Cheap, London, give interesting items of the cost of putting up a rood, and of demolishing it. 1553, " Item, paid for a new Rood with Mary and John, £7." 1558, " Item, paid for taking down the Rood and Mary and John, xx*d*."

Not infrequently, as at Lapford, Devon (100), Pulham St Mary, Norfolk, and Sherborne Minster, the eastern bays of the nave roof or vault received additional ornamentation as being the canopy above the head of the Crucified Saviour.

The Rood Beam

As we saw above (page 3), mention is made of a great beam of silver as having been given to Old St Peter's, Rome, by Pope Leo III. (795-816). It does not follow that it carried a rood. The rood or crucifix, at any rate a rood carrying an unclothed Christ, hardly appears before the eleventh century. It is possible that the beam at St Peter's carried nothing but lamps and candles. But we have definite mention of a rood with a Mary and John given to the abbey of Bury St Edmunds by Archbishop Stigand, just before or after the Norman Conquest (page 8); and an early mention of a rood beam occurs in the monk Gervase's account of Canterbury Cathedral before the fire of 1174, when "above the pulpitum, and placed across the quire, was a beam which sustained a great cross, two cherubim, and the images of St Mary and St John the Apostle."* This last was a quire screen. But roods are found in many other positions. At Headbourne Worthy, Hampshire, on the west wall of the nave, is an ancient Anglo-Saxon rood in stone. Another stone rood survives by the south door of Romsey nave.† Within

---

* "Pulpitum vero turrim (mediam) a navi quodammodo separabat. Supra pulpitum trabes erat per transversum ecclesiae posita, quæ crucem grandem et duo cherubim et imagines sanctæ Mariæ et sancti Johannis Apostoli sustentabat" (Willis' *Canterbury Cathedral*, 37).

† Externally, roods occur on a buttress near the west door of Sherborne,

Cullompton

a church the normal position for the rood is in front of the chancel arch. But mention is not wanting of roods in other positions, *e.g.*, of the following Kentish churches: Dartford had a rood on the south side of the church; St Mary-in-Hoo, on the north side; Halstow, at the font; Milton, on the south side of the chancel; Wateringbury, on the north side of the chancel door; Shorne, by the south door; Strood, at the pillar by the south door; West Wickham, by the north door.*

The rood beams were fixed in different ways. If the roof was one constructed with tie-beams, it was easy to arrange that one tie-beam should be fixed above the chancel arch close to the east wall of the nave. If it was a roof of a different type, a single tie-beam might nevertheless be introduced in this position; thus at Knapton, Norfolk,† though the roof is a hammerbeam one, it has at the east a tie-beam, which cuts right across the chancel arch. But in the majority of cases there was a loft or gallery above the screen, and this loft was made to serve as a substitute for the rood beam. Thus at Cullompton the rood was too huge and heavy to rest on a beam, so its foot was allowed to rest on the floor of the gallery or loft. At Cullompton it is carved out of the butts of two oak trees, measuring 9 feet 6 inches by 1 foot 6 inches by 1 foot 9 inches, and 6 feet by 1 foot 6 inches and 1 foot 9 inches; the base of the cross is carved to represent rocks, with skulls, crossed thigh bones, and shoulder blades upon them. In many wooden screens the horizontal timber on the top of the loft formed the beam to which the rood was fixed and tenoned. At Edington, Wilts, on the west front of the loft the woodwork is cut away in the centre, and again at equal distances on either side, probably for fixing the crucifix with its Mary and John. At Llanrwst the mortice holes are in the beam of the *eastern* parapet. In some cases the rood beam with its crucifix, Mary and John, was fixed above the loft, and independent of it. Sometimes, however, it is fixed so high up, at or above the apex of the chancel arch, that it is evident that the rood and images could not have been placed *on* it, they must have been suspended *from* it, *e.g.*, at Little Malvern and Cullompton. At Cullompton (104) we saw that the base of the crucifix was on the floor of the loft; on the east side of the beam high above is an iron stay, showing that the top

Dorset; over a south doorway of Burford, Oxon.; in the tower wall of St Lawrence, Evesham; 'on the Norman tympanum of the south door of Bolsover, Derbyshire; and at St Nicholas, Abingdon; Shipton Bellinger, Hants; Compton Bassett and Yatton Keynell, Wilts.

* Leland L. Duncan in *Parish Churches*, 246.
† Illustrated in *Gothic Architecture in England*, 567.

Kenton

arm of the cross was fastened there to the beam. At Banwell, Somerset, above the chancel arch is an angel which held a chain, from which the rood may have been suspended. At Cullompton the ends of the beam are borne by angels.* Most rood beams have disappeared, except where they formed part of the roof construction. Sometimes, however, the sawn-off ends may be seen, or the spot where they are plastered over, *e.g.*, at St Cross, Winchester, in the western arch of the central tower, and at Waltham Abbey, over the second pillars west of the east end of the nave; also at Fordwich and Igtham, Kent. At Exeter, the rood beam, strange to say, was of iron; in 1324 there is an entry for making it: "*in fac. ferr. portant. magnam crucem.*"† At Old Shoreham is a remarkable beam with the double billet moulding (date *c.* 1120) across the east wall of the nave. At Binsted, Sussex, the ends of another rood beam, richly moulded (date *c.* 1260), have been left sawn off in the wall.‡ Frequently the stone brackets remain, on which there rested either the rood beam or the "breastsummer" of the rood loft, *e.g.*, at Broadwater, Sussex (102).

The Rood Loft

It is beyond question, says Mr F. Bligh Bond,§ judging from the very large number of rood stairs and doorways still remaining, that "almost every church in Devonshire and the adjoining counties was once furnished with its rood loft and gallery front surmounting the chancel screen." In Lincolnshire alone, judging merely from the number of rood stairs and doorways remaining, there must have been more than a hundred rood lofts. It is hardly correct, however, to assume that every church had a rood loft; some screens, *e.g.*, such a screen as that of Great Bardfield (29), were so designed that it was difficult to superpose a rood loft on them.

Lofts seem not to have come into use in the parish churches till long after they were employed in the collegiate, cathedral, and monastic churches; in these last no doubt they were required by an elaborate ritual which was not in use in parish churches.

---

* Painted rood beams remain at Martham, Norfolk, Brabourne and Postling, Kent, and Ufford, Suffolk.

† Also in 1318 500 lbs. of iron were brought as ties to be used in the quire screen; "pro 500 lb. ferri ad faciend. magnas barras pro la pulpytte, 15s. 5d."

‡ Mr P. M. Johnston in *Victoria History of England*, ii. 357.

§ *Devonshire Screens*, 535.

Staverton

THE ROOD LOFT

They hardly appear in large parish churches before the fourteenth century, and in small ones not for another century.* After the Reformation few lofts were put up; a fine and late example remains at Rodney Stoke, Somerset (109). In France the rood screen with loft is called the "Jubé"; from the first words

Rodney Stoke

uttered by the gospeller: "Jube, Domine, benedicere." The reason why the gospel was read from on high, is definitely given by Pope Innocent III.; it is that they who tell the good tidings

* Dr E. Mansel Sympson (*Assoc. Societies' Reports*, xx. 189) mentions a rood-stairs doorway at Coltersworth, Lincolnshire, where the abacus of a jamb shaft has the nail-head ornament, and therefore presumably is of Norman date; but perhaps this is a case of reuse.

110   SCREENS AND GALLERIES

Astbury

of the gospel should go up on high, as said the prophet Isaiah (xl. 9):—

"Super montem excelsum ascende tu, qui evangelizas Sion, exalta in fortitudine vocem tuam."

In breadth the loft platforms were generally about 6 feet, but they vary from 5 feet to as much as the 8 feet of Minehead. The sides of the platform were protected by parapets, usually of openwork. In the noblest examples, *e.g.*, in the surviving lofts of Llanrwst, Denbigh (82), and Atherington, Devon (43), the western parapet of the loft was constructed in nichework, on the back of each niche being painted figures of apostles, saints, and bishops, or else the niches were filled with wooden statuettes. In humbler churches, where the chancel arch was low, the loft had only a western parapet, the wall carried by the chancel arch serving as an eastern parapet; *e.g.*, at St Margaret's (112).

The methods of supporting a loft varied. When in each bay of the screen there was a pointed arch, the loft could be, and usually was, coved on either side or supported by a semi-vault, either a lierne vault, as at Mobberley, Cheshire (45), or a fan vault, as at High Ham, Somerset (65);* and on these covings or semi-vaults were poised the floor and parapets of the loft. But if the bays consisted of square-headed windows, as they sometimes did, coving and vaulting were impossible. Early examples of coving and vaulting are seen on the screens of Halberton and Uffculme, Devon, *c.* 1420. In Norfolk and Suffolk, when the lofts and organs were taken down, the coving and groining was often removed at the same time; in Devon it was usually spared. At Bridford, Devon (138), the coving has been destroyed, and bits of it have been nailed against the spandrels. A much simpler method, adapted for poor parishes, was to support

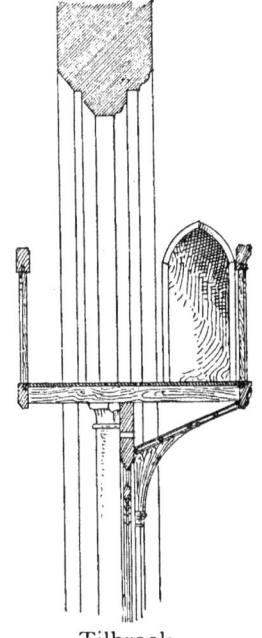

Tilbrook

* This cantilever arrangement is shown in the drawing of Tilbrook, Hunts (111), where, if the vaulting ribs were omitted, what would be left would be coving: the difference between the two is that one professes to be vaulting, while the other does not. *Cf.* the drawing of Llanegryn screen (178).

Church Handborough

St Margaret's

the loft partly on the east wall of the nave, partly on posts and beam a little farther west. This is the case at Greywell, Hants, where the screen is placed six feet west of the chancel arch, and at St Margaret's, Herefordshire (112). A common arrangement was to fix a stout beam parallel to the top beam of the screen, some two feet westward of it, and on these two beams to support the loft. This method is employed at Church Handborough, Oxon. (112), Hubberholme and Flamborough, Yorkshire (132). A more elaborate method was to construct two entirely indepen-

Milborne Port

dent screens five or six feet apart, and connect them by a ceiling. This is seen at Edington, Wilts, and at Montgomery. It is translated into stone in most delightful fashion at Compton Bassett, Wilts (35), where the front screen consists of three open arches, of which the two lateral ones serve as altar recesses, while in the rear screen is a doorway flanked by square-headed windows.*

* The loft of this screen had originally stone parapets like those of Tattershall; these were replaced by balustrades of wood, which were destroyed at "restoration."

114   SCREENS AND GALLERIES

Westham

Greenhithe

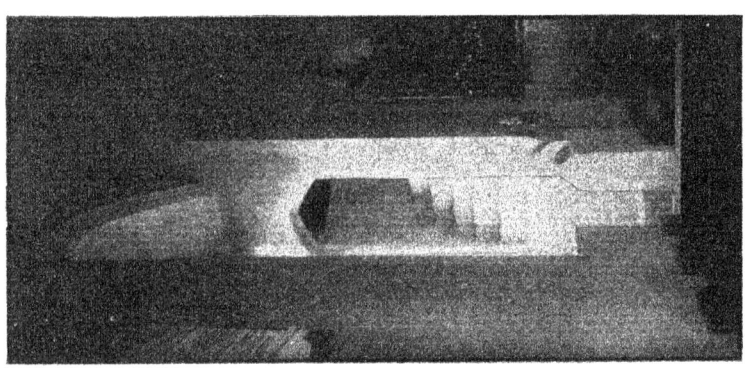

Wingfield

THE ROOD LOFT

The lofts were usually reached by staircases. If the church was small there might be a staircase inside one of the piers of the chancel arch, or inside both piers as at Wiggenhall St Mary Magdalen, Norfolk. If the lofts passed across the aisles there might be a staircase in one of the aisle walls, *e.g.*, at Covehithe (114), or in both as at Wingfield (114) and Dennington (14), Suffolk. Sometimes, as at Westham, Sussex (114), there was a staircase turret outside one aisle wall, or a turret outside each of the aisle walls. It is clear from the doorways shown at Dennington, Suffolk, where the aisles retain both their screens and lofts, and elsewhere, that the eastern screens of the eastern bay of the aisles were not always in a line with the screen across the chancel arch, but were one bay west of it. The doorway of the rood stairs is usually quite plain, but an enriched example, with crocketed hood-mold and finial, occurs at St Alphege, Canterbury. The doors of rood stairs remain, by exception, at Shoreham, Kent, Blewbury, Berkshire (116), and a few other places. It by no means follows that where a rood screen existed, it was always approached by stairs. There are many churches which undoubtedly possessed lofts, but which show no signs of staircases, *e.g.*, Hubberholme. In such cases the loft must have been approached either by a ladder or by movable wooden steps. Sometimes a doorway is seen, so high up, *e.g.*, at Cirencester* and Berkeley, that it hardly seems likely that it gave access to the loft. Perhaps it was there to facilitate the drawing up of the rood cloth or veil (page 9).† Sometimes the spiral staircase or "vice" was carried up so as to form a turret projecting above the roof, *e.g.*, Grantham, Lincolnshire, and Westham, Kent (114). Some churches have a pair of these rood turrets, one alongside each aisle wall. The rood turret was sometimes utilised as a belfry for the sacring bell, *e.g.*, at Sedgebrook, Lincolnshire. ‡ Sometimes it was merely an easy method of access to the roofs.§

Where there is or was a rood loft, it will sometimes be found, if the easternmost arch of the nave be examined, that its two sides do not correspond, the easternmost being the highest at the springing ; *e.g.*, at Sittingbourne, Kent, the eastern side of the

---

* Illustrated in *Gothic Architecture in England*, 544.

† High doorways may occur in other positions. At St Mary Redcliffe is a high doorway under the clerestory-sill (there is no triforium) on either side of the last bay of the chancel. This may have been to get access to a gallery running across the chancel at the back of the reredos, so as to light candles, or else to an altar beam.

‡ *Assoc. Societies' Reports*, xx. 189.

§ See illustration of Maxey (122) for rood stairs continuing higher up than the loft doorway.

116   SCREENS AND GALLERIES

Whaplode

Blewbury

arch was taken down and made rampant by large new voussoirs cut to a different sweep, so that the two sides rise from different levels. The higher spring on the eastern side allowed headway for a tall rood loft.* Wherever such a distorted arch remains, even if there is now no sign of rood stairs, it is proof positive that there once existed a big loft stretching all the way across the church, *e.g.*, at Stockton, Wilts (27). At Erith the distortion is so great as to be a positive deformity; but it was, of course, invisible so long as the rood loft remained.† In 1480, William Finch of Lynsted left the following direction in his will:—" Item lego versus facturam unius arche de novo faciendi in ecclesia parochiali de Lyngsted, 13s. 4d." Mr Aymer Vallance suggests that it was to build the distorted eastern arch still to be seen at Lynsted that this money was left. One method to get a continuous screen across an aisled nave was, as has been shown, to tilt up the easternmost arch. If, however, there was a large eastern respond to the nave arcade, a doorway could be cut through the respond, so as to allow passage from the loft in front of the chancel arch to the loft at the end of the aisle. Doorways in this position may often be seen, *e.g.*, at Dartford, Kent. In the Stratton contract (page 41), it is particularly specified that a way is to be made for the loft "by or under the arches" of the pier arcade. At Maxey (122), another curious change has occurred. In the thirteenth century the chancel arch evidently descended much lower, down to the thirteenth-century capital shown in the illustration. It was not till the loft was built, whose former presence is proved by the loft doorway and piscina still remaining, that it was stilted as we see it now.

In a church without a chancel arch, and with eastern as well as western aisles, the piers were usually allowed to cut the screen across the three naves into three sections, *e.g.*, at Wolborough, Devon (20). But in rich examples the piers were sometimes cased in, so as not to interfere with the continuity of the screen and loft design. Such casings or panellings are seen, of simple character, at Staverton, Devon (108); more enriched, at Dunchideock, Devon (118), and quite gorgeous at Harberton, Devon (12), where they almost look as if they might have served as reredoses for lateral altars.

A fair number of lofts remain *in situ*. Among the best is the fragment at Atherington, Devon, remaining over the north

---

* Dr Francis Grayling in *Arch. Cantiana*, xxiii. 150.

† Other Kentish examples are—Biddenden, Lynsted, Staplehurst, Cranbrook, and Goudhurst. The arches also of Hartland, Devon, have been reset to make room for a loft. For Erith see illustration in *Arch. Cantiana*, xvi. 156.

118   SCREENS AND GALLERIES

aisle (43). At Marwood, Devon, only the eastern parapet remains; it therefore does not appear in the illustration, which is taken from the west. At Tattershall, Lincolnshire, is a fine stone quire screen; the inscription is preserved by Holles: "*Orate pro anima Roberti de Whalley hujus collegii, qui hoc opus fieri fecit Anno Donini* MCCCCCXXVIII., *cujus animæ prospicietur Deus. Amen.*" In this example there is a staircase at the north end, and a projection in the loft to the east, in which are two book-rests; the parapets of the loft consist of solid walls 4 feet 7 inches high.* As a rule the western parapet is more enriched than the eastern, as may be seen by comparing the two illustrations of Llanrwst † (82), but in some cases the tabernacle work of the western front has been so much mutilated in removing images or defacing paintings, that it is now the plainer of the two.

The loft was of great service in many ways. As we have seen, it often served to support the rood and the Mary and John, and also lamp-bowls and candlesticks, and made it easier to attend to the different lights. It also supported reliquaries. On the parclose screens of Winchester Cathedral still rest chests containing relics of bygone Anglo-Saxon kings and saints. It facilitated the veiling of the rood, Mary, and John by the "rood cloth," which was drawn up by cords in front of the rood loft.

The fabric rolls of York Minster for 1518 record payments "for painting of one cloth to hang before the new crucifix in the time of Lent, 10s.; and for colours for painting the newly made canvas, 8d.; and for the curtain rings, and for the lace, and for sewing the cloth, 12s.; and for one hundred fathoms of cord for suspending the linen cloth in Lent before the crucifix, 4s." ‡

Some of the lofts have projections in the centre of the eastern or the western side, or both.§ Some contain lecterns. These are still left in many churches on the Continent; they were either movable brass stands, like those in quires, or marble desks, forming part of the masonry of the design. Those at the Erari at Venice are most beautiful; ‖ and to come nearer home, in a rood loft at Tattershall Church is a curiously moulded stone desk for the reader of the lessons. At Priziac, Morbihan, is a

* Dr E. Mansel Sympson in *Proceedings of Society of Antiquaries*, 28th March 1901.

† Several lofts have been replaced lately, *e.g.*, those of Lew Trenchard Kenton, and Staverton, Devon, under the direction of Mr F. Bligh Bond.

‡ Browne's *York Minster*, 270.

§ *E.g.*, Tattershall, Spalding, and Cotes-by-Stow (120), Lincolnshire; Mobberley, Cheshire (45); Dunster, Somerset; Lullingstone, Kent; Montgomery; Newark.

‖ F. F. Fox, *Bristol and Gloucester A.S.*, xxiii.

Cotes-by-Stow

reading desk in the form of a swan placed over the eastern side of the loft. The projections might be intended as pulpits, or they may have been occupied by the organ. The lecterns may have been intended for a reader or a preacher, or merely to hold the organist's music; this last was certainly the case at St Stephen, Walbrook, London, where there was "a stondying lecterne for to ley on a boke to play with." It has been argued that it is very improbable that the gospel, or the epistle and gospel, were read from the rood loft, or that sermons were preached from it in *parish* churches, because the rood stairs are usually so narrow that a stout man could hardly scrape along them, and a vested priest would seriously damage his costly chasuble. This objection, however, may be dismissed, for it is quite certain that in several cases there was an altar in the loft, and if the priest found his way to celebrate at the altar, he could do so also to read the epistle or gospel. In any case it does not follow that he would have to mount the narrow staircase in vestments; he might vest in the loft. The documentary evidence, however, as to the use of the loft by the priest is not conclusive. At Wingham, near Sandwich, certain things are recorded to have occurred "when the priest had read the gospel *in the rood läft*"; but Wingham was a collegiate church, so that the reference is not to the point. At Long Melford, Suffolk, it is recorded that "on Good Friday a priest then standing *by* the rood sang the passion"; but this does not necessarily mean that he was standing on the rood loft.

Another supposition is that the loft was used for preaching purposes. It is pointed out that in several examples, *e.g.*, Mobberley, Cheshire (45), Spalding, and Cotes-by-Stow, Lincolnshire (120), there are central bays in the rood lofts projecting westward. At Montgomery, Tattershall, and Dunster, however, where also there are central projecting bays, they face the chancel; even if in the former they were pulpits, in the latter they could not be. Moreover, if the rood loft was pulpit, why at the same time put up a grand pulpit on the nave floor, as was sometimes done, *e.g.*, at Nantwich, Cheshire, where the rood loft and the pulpit were designed and erected together. Also pulpits were put up long after lofts had come into use; in these cases certainly the lofts can hardly have been used as pulpits. After the Reformation, however, there are instances of the pulpit use of lofts. In at least two Devonshire parishes sermons were preached from the rood loft till a comparatively recent date.

There is also reason to believe that the Blessed Sacrament was sometimes exposed either on the rood loft, or on an altar upon or attached to the chancel screen; but these expositions were only at considerable intervals of time, being only permitted on some great and urgent occasion, when they were conducted with the greatest possible solemnity.*

Another use of the loft, as surprising as it is undoubted, was to support an altar. So that the rood loft was at times a chapel. At York Minster there were two chantries "at the altar of the Saviour in the little rood loft." Dr Cox quotes an endowment at Grantham in 1349 for masses to be said "in solario (*i.e.*, the loft) before the great rood in the midst of the church, after the first stroke of the day bell." Some of the eastward or westward projections of the screens may have been to carry altars, not organs. At Little Hereford, Herefordshire, there is a piscina in the loft in a position which argues a *central* altar. Numerous piscinas or traces of piscinas in lofts or high up in the jambs of chancel arches remain.† At Westminster there is known to have been an altar in the rood loft; it was called the altar of St Paul and the Crucifix; to which, for kissing the feet of the rood, the people ascended the steps on the left on one side, and descended on the other. ‡

Maxey

One other use of the loft is beyond question, viz., that it held

* Mr F. F. Fox, xxiii. 89.
† *E.g.*, Bilton, Warwick; Bitton, Gloucester; Brownsover, Warwick; Burghill, Hereford; Church Lawford, Warwick; Deddington, Oxon.; Great Hallingbury, Essex; Horningsea, Cambridge; Maxey, Northants (122); New Shoreham, Sussex; Oddington, Oxon.; Ross, Hereford; Tenby, Pembroke; Wigmore, Hereford.
‡ Lethaby's *Westminster*, 26.

the village organ, the village organist, and the village quire. No tramp of gospeller or preacher could have worn the steps of the rood staircases to the state we so often find them in. In some the steps have had to be replaced; at Horning, Norfolk, by Purbeck marble. It was the hob-nailed boots or the clogs of the village boys that did this.* In 1473 there was paid in an Exeter church " for making a seat in le roode-lofte, when playing on the organys . . . 7s." The following entry occurs in an inventory of St Stephen, Walbrook, London:—" In the same rood loft is a pair of organs, and a lid over the keys with lock and key, the gift of Borton Wyvis, grocer. Also a stool to sit on when he playeth on the organs." In the collegiate church of Tattershall the screen still carries the organ, just as in Exeter Cathedral. A new rood loft was built about 1444 in St Mary's, Sandwich; organs were placed in it, and the parish paid various sums to musical priests for playing these organs. At Louth there was paid in 1509, " for setting of the Flemish organ in the rood loft by four days . . . xx$d$." It would almost appear as if the Church of England services in the fifteenth and sixteenth centuries became more choral than ever before, so numerous are the references to rood organs and rood lecterns in wills and churchwardens' accounts.†
So popular were rood lofts, that in spite of all injunctions many churches retained them till quite lately. That at Chedzoy, Somerset, was not moved to the west of the nave till 1841; that at Wigan was not removed till 1847; that at Manchester, not till 1860; the Jacobean loft at Circencester was demolished at a recent restoration. New lofts were also put up here and there after the Reformation, no doubt as choir galleries, *e.g.*, in 1610 at Wimborne Minster. The Jacobean loft at Rodney Stoke (109) remained in use as the singers' gallery till *c.* 1850.

One further use of the loft is beyond question, but it is a post-Reformation use. The richest or most influential parishioner who could get possession of it, sometimes used it as a pew; there he sat with his back to the altar. At Bradnich, Devon, the last proprietor of the pew in the rood loft was an old lady who used to get up to it by a step ladder. Pews were inserted in the loft at Minehead in 1630; these remained in use by the school

* And when they turned sleepy, they leant back on their benches against the parapets of the choir, and these became rickety, and for that reason have often been taken down.

† Mr Micklethwaite's view was, that "the spread of rood lofts in this country may be ascribed chiefly to the increasingly choral nature of the services before the Reformation," and "is established beyond possibility of doubt." "Even the smallest parish churches had a gallery on the chancel screen. This was used for the 'minstrels,' vocal and instrumental, hired by the rich parishes on high days."

124 SCREENS AND GALLERIES

Wenhaston

children till 1887. The loft pew at St Mary, Taunton, was only demolished recently. Unfortunately, with these pews, the screens also have in most cases been demolished, or have been replaced in cheap and nasty varnished pitch pine. At Lastingham, Yorkshire, some repairs to the roof being necessary, the churchwardens made a fire of the screen to melt the lead.*

TYMPANIC SCREENS; THE COMMANDMENTS; THE ROYAL ARMS

It has been shown above (pages 24 and 28), that among the types of screens executed in stone are two, those of which Westwell (23) and Sandridge (28) are examples, in which the separation of chancel from nave is effected by a solid wall carried right up to the gable. There were also churches, *e.g.*, Eartham (27), which retained a primitive small and low chancel arch, carrying a great space of wall. This upper expanse of plain wall invited mural painting, and, no doubt, often received it. At Wingerworth, Derbyshire, some forty years ago, the outlines of the great rood, with the attendant figures that had originally stood there, could be plainly seen.† What was done at Wingerworth in stone, was done very commonly elsewhere in wood. All that was necessary was to continue the eastern parapet of the rood loft upwards till it reached the apex of the chancel arch; or, if there was no chancel arch, till it reached the gable. Strange as it may seem to us that the chancel arches should be boarded up, making of the chancel a chapel of which only the merest glimpses could be obtained from the nave, there can be no doubt that the practice was quite common; for it is found in districts so wide apart as Devon, Somerset, Hampshire, Wiltshire, Leicestershire, Essex, Norfolk, Suffolk, Sussex, and Wales; *e.g.*, Bettws Newydd (179), and Bradwell, near

* Good examples of lofts remain at Atherington, Devon; Amesbury and Avebury, Wilts; Edington, Wilts; Flamborough, Yorkshire; Hillesden, Bucks; Hubberholme, Yorks, 1558 (measured drawing in *Architectural Association Sketch Book*, 3, v. 27); Marwood, Devon; Rodney Stoke, Somerset; St John's Timberhill, Norwich (sketch by Sir Charles Nicholson in *Architectural Association Sketch Book*, 3, i. 55); Sheringham, Norfolk; South Warnborough, Hants; Tattershall, Lincolnshire; Tilbrook, Hants; Warfield, Berks (measured drawing in *Spring Gardens Sketch Book*, v. 63), and several in Wales.

† Dr Cox, *Churches of Derbyshire*, i. 449. At Hoo, Kent, a bequest was made in 1493 for painting a doom over the rood (*Testamenta Cantiana*, xi.).

126 SCREENS AND GALLERIES

Bradwell

Coggeshall (126). Here, above all, was introduced into the old churches the potent element of "mystery." The most important example surviving is that at Wenhaston, Suffolk (124).*

An important part of the "restoration" of Wenhaston was the removal of the partition which separated the chancel from the nave, and accordingly this was taken down and placed in the churchyard. During the night a heavy shower of rain washed off some of the layers of plaster and exposed to view a portion of the panel with parts of the figures of the Blessed Virgin and St John the Baptist upon it. Information was at once given to the vicar, under whose direction the boards were carefully washed, and a missing portion searched for and found among the *débris*. The whole was then carefully put together and set up in the old schoolroom close by, and as the result we have one of the most interesting panel paintings which have been noted in recent times. The size of the picture is 8 feet 6 inches in height in the centre, by 17 feet 3 inches in the broadest part, and it is painted on a series of boards, which appear to have been partly bonded together by the representation of the holy rood affixed to them. This has entirely disappeared, but the outline of a large cross ragulé in the centre, with a figure on either side, is clearly discernible. The cross, on which no doubt hung a figure of our Saviour, occupies nearly the whole height of the picture, with widely extended arms, while the figures of the Blessed Virgin and St John the Evangelist on either side were about 4 feet 6 inches high. The whole of the intervening and surrounding spaces are occupied with the subject of the Doom. The painting is in distemper. The general groundwork of the picture has been olive-green, and a considerable variety of colouring has been used in depicting the several portions of the subject. In the upper part is a figure of our Blessed Lord seated on the rainbow. He has dark hair and a star-like nimbus, the gilding on which was very distinct when first brought to light. A bright red mantle is thrown loosely round the body so as to leave the right side bare. He has the two fingers of the right hand extended in the attitude of benediction, and drops of blood are falling from the wounds in the hand and right side. Above his head is a representation of the sun, and from his right hand proceeds a scroll, no doubt with the inscription "Venite Benedicti," but no trace of this now remains. In a corresponding position on the sinister side of the cross is a kneeling figure of the Blessed Virgin, also with dark hair and golden nimbus, but not crowned. She has a red cloak and blue

* Wenhaston is fully described and illustrated by Mr C. E Keyser in *Archæologia*, liv., from which the following description is abridged.

dress somewhat faded, and her hands are raised in a supplicating attitude. Behind her, and kneeling with hands raised towards the great Judge is a figure, also nimbed, with dark hair and beard, a coarse yellow garment and bare legs, doubtless intended for St John the Baptist, who is not often represented as an intercessor. Above the head of the Virgin is the moon, and at the side a scroll. Below the figures of the Virgin and St John the Baptist is the subject of the Weighing of Souls. A majestic figure of St Michael with dark hair and extended wings, cross on his forehead, red mantle and white vestments, holds the sword of justice in his right hand and the balances in his left. In the sinister scale are two small demons, while the good deeds of the soul which is being weighed are as usual portrayed by a small naked figure in the dexter scale. On the south side is a large portraiture of Lucifer or Satan, a black demon with horns and diabolical features, a pair of bat's wings, long tail, and eye in his belly. On the opposite side of the cross is another group, namely, St Peter receiving four figures who have safely passed through the ordeal of soul-weighing. St Peter is very richly attired in full ecclesiastical vestments and with triple papal tiara. He holds a large key in his hand, and is receiving the four figures at the gate of Heaven. These figures are all naked, but are distinguished by crowns, a mitre, and a cardinal's hat; they therefore represent a king, queen, bishop, and cardinal. All have their hands raised in adoration. The flesh tints are very delicate and perfect, as in all the nude figures in the picture. Left of these are the heavenly mansions, which have two doorways, at each of which an angel is admitting a nude figure.* On the extreme right are the jaws of Hell, portrayed, as usual, by the head of an immense fish with gaping jaws. Within the jaws is a black demon seizing the leg of a nude prostrate figure with dark hair and dragging him in, while eight more figures, one at least a female, are encircled by a pale red chain, probably suggestive of its being red hot, and are being forced into the abyss. All the figures of this group have black or dark-brown hair, nor is there a single figure in any of the groups with the golden hair met with in most of the mural paintings in our English churches. Above are five figures rising from their graves, all facing towards the cross, and in varied attitudes of devotion. The general treatment of the subject, the architecture of the heavenly mansions, and such distinctive features as the tiara of St Peter, and the crowns, mitre, and cardinal's hat of the figures before him, all prove the work to have been executed between 1500 and 1538. This tympanum now stands in the western gallery of Wenhaston Church.

The treatment of the boarded tympanum was probably not always the same. Sometimes probably the rood, Mary, and John might be merely painted on it; but at Wenhaston and probably at Dauntsey, all three were in wood, carved in three-quarter relief, and pegged on to the boarding of the tympanum.* Sometimes, the better to light the paintings on the tympanum, a small window was inserted in the nave wall close to the wall-plate. Such a one exists at Wenhaston (150). Another is shown in an old print of the north side of Shere

Wickhamford

Church, Surrey; at a "restoration" it has been rebuilt in "Early English," in ignorance of or indifference to its history. In the Stratton contract quoted on page 41, two windows are to be inserted in the nave roof above the crucifix. At Welsh Newton, Herefordshire, is a dormer window which would

* The following tympanic screens remain :—In Devon, Molland Bottreux and Parracombe ; in Somerset, Raddington and Winsham ; in Gloucester, Mitcheldean ; in Hampshire, Ellingham ; in Wiltshire, Dauntsey ; in Leicestershire, Lockington ; in Essex, Bradwell near Coggeshall ; in Norfolk, Ludham ; in Suffolk, Wenhaston ; in Wales, Bettws Newydd, Llanelieu, Brecknock, and others. In Sussex they existed at Henfield, Ifield, Rusper, Warringhurst, and Racton ; at Treyford and Barnham they came down to the ground (*Victoria History of Sussex*, vol. ii.). At St Michael's Church, St Albans, part of the tympanum has been removed to the vestry. See *Suffolk Arch. Institute*, viii. 242 ; *Bristol and Gloucester Arch. Soc.*, vi. 262 ; and Robinson's *History of Enfield*, ii. 8.

Rowston

Welsh Newton

serve very well to light a Doom (130). When the Reformation arrived, the Reformers did not always carry out the injunctions so far as to destroy both the rood and the tympanum; sometimes they retained the latter but turned it to better use. The better use was obtained by removing from it the carved rood, Mary and John, and by defacing, and as far as possible erasing, the paintings on it. Sometimes the old tympanum was covered with canvas on which were painted godly texts and the like.* Mr Daniel-Tyssen quotes an entry anent Wandsworth in the *Surrey Inventories* for 1552: "Paid for pulling down the rood loft and setting up of the Scriptures, that is to say, the Creation of the World, the Coming of our Saviour Christ, the Beatitudes, the Ten Commandments, the Twelve Articles of our Belief, and the Lord's Prayer, the Judgment of the World, the King's Majesty's Arms, iv*l.* xii*s.* vi*d.*" This introduction of the Commandments into churches was no new or Protestant usage, for in pre-Reformation wills bequests occur for setting up the Commandments. They were, however, specially commended to the parishes in 1560 by Queen Elizabeth, perhaps because the tympana and the walls generally had become unsightly by the recent scraping or destruction of paintings on walls and tympana; for the commissioners specially animadvert on those who spare no cost on their private houses, but in God's house permit "open decaies and ruins of coveringes, walls and wyndowes, and   . leave the place of prayers desolate of all meet ornaments for such a place." Ludlow retains a table of the Commandments put up the very next year; it is on a panel; the accounts for 1561 specify moneys paid among other things "for the table of commaundments." Elizabethan tables of the Commandments remain at Aylmerton, Norfolk, painted on boards and affixed to the east wall of the nave. In Bengeworth, Gloucester, is a table of the Commandments, cut in boxwood, and dated 1591. In Queen Mary's reign it was attempted to reverse all this. Pugin notes that in one instance the cloth painted with the Commandments was taken down and cut into surplices. In the accounts for Ashburton parish in 1554 is the entry, "Striking out of the Scripture upon the Rood Loft, vi*d.*" On Mary's death her wishes became of no effect, and tables of the Commandments were set up in the churches almost universally. Sometimes they took the form of frescoes; several examples of the Commandments, the Lord's Prayer, and a collect remain in admirable lettering, *e.g.*, on the

* Wickhamford, Worcester (129), has the royal arms painted on an older tympanum. Archbishop Sandys is said to have brought the woodwork of this church from one of the city churches in London.

Flamborough

east walls of the transepts of Terrington St Clement, Norfolk, 1635 (133). As to the position of the table of the Commandments, it is asserted that it was intended to be set up on the east wall of the nave. Elizabeth's Commissioners, however, in 1560, ordered it " to be comely set up or hung up in the east end of the

Terrington St Clement

chancel"; and this was repeated in the Articles of 1564. So also at Bristol " the table of the comandts. was to be painted in large caracters on the east end of the quier whear the comu. table usually doth stande." Nevertheless, in some cases the table was set up on the east wall of the nave, *e.g*, at Flamborough, Yorkshire (132), partly because, where the screen was

Wells, St Cuthbert

Harberton

retained, the table would have been almost invisible if placed at the far end of the chancel; partly perhaps, because, where the tympanum had been scraped and retained, something was wanted to take off from its plainness and bareness.

The chancel arch was also the favourite position for the royal arms. The royal arms were set up even as early as Henry VIII.'s reign. They appeared on the magnificent screen (1543-47) in the cathedral, which the Bristol people demolished with the aid of eminent architects in 1860; and at Bletchingley, Surrey, there was paid in 1546 "vi/. xvs. iid. for painting the quire and the rood loft, the *king's arns*, the outer quire, aisle, etc." In 1547 the Long Melford churchwardens paid for painting the arms of Edward VI.* The Tudor arms were a lion and a greyhound, and bitter were the allusions to the change in the polite controversies of the theologians. "If you mark the devil's language well," says Dr Martin to Dr Cranmer in 1556, "it agrees with your proceedings most truly." "*Mitte de deorsum*," "Cast thyself down," saith the devil. " Down with the sacrament, down with the mass, down with the altars, down with the arms of Christ, and up with a lion and a dog." And Dr Harding asks Dr Jewell, "Is it the word of God setteth up a dog and a dragon in the place of the Blessed Virgin Mary, Mother of God, and St John the Evangelist, which were wont to stand on either side of Christ crucified?" "It was like a declaration on their part," said another, "that they were worshippers, not of our Lord, whose image they had contemptuously thrown aside, but of an earthly king whose armorial bearings they had substituted for it." In 1660 it was made compulsory to put up the royal arms. and from that date onward numerous examples are to be found, or were to be found till recently.†

* In 1612 the churchwardens of Melton Mowbray paid "for lyme and workmanship aboute kinges armes ijs. iiijd."
† In 1882 Mr Bloxam noted the following :—The arms of *Queen Elizabeth* at St Martin and St Thomas, Salisbury ; St Michael's, Coventry ; and Sandford, Oxon. ; of *James I.* at Wyke Chapel, Champflower, Somerset ; of *Charles I.* at Broadway, Gloucester ; Beverley Minster ; St Alban's ; Haltham, Lincoln ; Aylmerton, Norfolk ; of the *Commonwealth* at Anstey, Warwick ; of *Charles II.* at Monks Kirby, Warwick ; Huish Episcopi, Langport, and Curry Revell, Somerset ; Ightham, Kent ; Loughborough, and Market Harborough, Leicester ; and Normanton, Notts (all these four in plaster) ; Burton Overy, Leicester (carved in wood) ; Over Compton, Dorset ; and Blundeston, Suffolk ; of *James II.* at Packwood, Warwick ; Grafton Flyford, Worcester ; and Oulton, Suffolk ; of *William III.* at Brympton, Somerset ; Saxlingham, Norfolk ; Fleet, Lincoln ; Yarmouth, Norfolk ; of *Anne* at Gedney, Lincoln ; Ledsham, Yorkshire ; South Petherton, Somerset ; St Benedict's, Norwich ; Lockington, Leicester (plaster) ; of *George I.* at Yarmouth, Isle of Wight ; Churchover, Warwick ; Trunch, Norfolk ; Brailes, Warwick ; of *George II.* at Wysall, Notts ; Waghen-on-Wawne,

TOWER SCREENS

In a small number of churches the arch of the western tower is fenced off by a screen.* That at Brightlingsea, Essex, was put up late in the fifteenth century; that at Worstead (136) in 1550.† There are others at Heckington, Lincolnshire, Harlestone, Norfolk, and elsewhere. There appear to be none in Devon, except such as have been removed to the west in modern times. The platform inside has been supposed to be for the ringers. But as they had already a ringers' chamber higher up, it is more likely that it was provided for the village choir deposed from its ancient position in the rood loft.‡ If so, it is the ancestor of the Elizabethan and Jacobean western galleries which were soon afterwards built in front of the tower arch, sometimes stretching across the aisles.

Worstead

Yorks; Normanton, Derbyshire. The series goes on with the usual unbroken continuity of English institutions to *Victoria*, with the date 1852, at Oddicombe, Somerset, the only break being that of *Queen Mary*, 1553-1558: a fine chain of witnesses to the Erastianism of the Reformed Church; bringing the history of the choir screen, which commenced in the third up to the middle of the nineteenth century.

* In some cases there is now neither screen nor floor, but a doorway remains high up in the tower wall, which originally gave access to a floor.

† "The screen was erected in 1831. Previously the balustrade of 1550 was supported by a four-centred arch, as old engravings show; *if* Cawston."—W. D.

‡ The gallery of the Winterborne Abbas band (page 145) was under the tower.

Destruction of Screens

Such then is the history of the decline and fall of the screen—of all the accessories of the mediæval church the most beautiful. The first step was the order of 1547 to destroy all images. The result of this was that every rood in the country, with its attendant images of Mary and John, was removed; of all the roods only two small and rude fragments survive.

> "They plucked down the rood from the screen,
> And flung to the moles and the bats,
> Then capered like goats on the green,
> And tossed up their greasy old hats."

In 1561, the second year of Queen Elizabeth, the rood lofts were attacked. But considerable liberty as to the lofts was left to the parishes. They might be destroyed, and, indeed, in 1560 "was alle the rood loftes taken down in London"* Whenever there came a Puritan bishop, as to the diocese of Norwich, a special mark of his reforming energy was the destruction of every loft he could hear of. Sometimes advantage was taken of the permission specially reserved to "transpose" or shift the lofts; they were moved to the west end of the church and became western choir galleries.† Sometimes the loft was destroyed and its coved supports as well. In such a case new cresting had to be put on the screen. That is the reason why not infrequently the cresting is of later date than the screen beneath it; thus occasionally there is found Jacobean cresting on a Gothic screen. In a certain Devonshire parish the cresting is of cast iron. It was, indeed, specially ordered that when the loft was taken down the screen should receive a new cresting. In 1576 Archbishop Grindal asks, "Whether your rood lofts be . . . altered, so that the upper part thereof with the soller or loft be quite taken down unto the cross-beam, and that the said beam have some convenient *crest*

---

* In that year the screen of St Dunstan's, Canterbury, fetched 17s., less 3s. 4d. for cost of pulling it down (Mr A. Vallance, 103).

† "At Strensham, Worcester (140), the western singing gallery is the old chancel screen of the sixteenth century. In the panels are twenty-three painted figures. Our Lord in glory occupies the central panel. On either side are the apostles. On our Lord's extreme right are two archbishops —one of them perhaps St Thomas of Canterbury, the other St Oswald of Worcester—St John Baptist, St Blaise, and St Edmund Martyr. On the extreme left is a bishop, a king, St Laurence and St Stephen, and St Anthony with his pig and staff. The supporters in the royal arms at Berkeley Castle chapel (142) are those used by Henry VII. and Henry VIII. See *Bristol and Gloucester Arch. Soc.* for 1904, p. 9."—Dr Oscar Clark.

Bridford

put upon the same?" Sometimes the coving as well as the loft was removed, and bits of the old coving were used to fill up the spandrels. This explains such awkward combinations as one sees in the screen of Bridford (138), Devon. In 1644 the Commonwealth promulgated an ordinance that all roods, fonts, and organs should not only be taken away, but should be defaced. This was not universally obeyed, but it brought destruction on many lofts; indeed the removal of the organ would in many cases involve the destruction of the loft. And as time went on, where the loft remained in use as a singing gallery, in many a case it needed repairs which no living man was competent to execute, even if the parish had been willing to disburse the very large amount of money required. Especially was this the case where the Sunday school was seated in it, and, said the churchwarden, "the children did kick it to pieces." In the end very few rood lofts survived. As for the screens, there never yet has been a legal order enjoining or permitting the destruction of a screen. It is just as much rank contempt of the law to destroy a screen —one vicar in the last century had the destruction of three on his conscience—as it is to destroy the font or the altar, or anything else. A faculty is necessary if a screen is to be destroyed. Nevertheless hundreds of ancient screens have perished in recent times. Sometimes the traceried panels got out of repair and all the beautiful upper part of the screen was cut away, leaving only the solid panels below, as in the truncated screen, once so glorious, of the great parish church of North Walsham. And what mediæval screens are left are fast being wrecked by irresponsible vicars' wives and curates. Many now bristle with nails and tin tacks, the wood being bruised and chipped and pierced and split in a way that no lady would dream of allowing any one to treat the furniture in her own private house;* but such treatment, it seems, is good enough for the House of God. In those churches which possessed parochial altars in the nave, and of which the quire had not been destroyed, it is possible that sometimes the destruction of this nave altar brought about the destruction of all barriers between its site and the high altar in the quire. In these, so long as the pulpitum or the rood screen was allowed to stand, the quire services were altogether invisible to the congregation, as they are still to this day at Canterbury and York (154), and wherever else either of these screens has been allowed to remain. Most of the greater churches, however, have been content to adhere to the ancient and proper practice, that they should retain the division into two separate churches—one

* *Memorials of Old Kent*, 44.

140 SCREENS AND GALLERIES.

Strensham

the private chapel of the dean and chapter, the other the church of the laity. Others, for congregational purposes, have preferred to turn the cathedral into a parish church; this has been done quite recently at St Paul's. It was this congregational ideal probably which brought about the awful destruction of screens in the French cathedrals. Out of some 250 French cathedrals now only one, Albi, has its western choir screen *in situ ;* that is because of the curious arrangement by which at Albi there is an altar at each end of the cathedral—the canon's altar to the east, and the parochial altar to the west, the clergy and laity worshipping back to back. Most of this destruction in France took place in the eighteenth century, stone screens being replaced by iron railings.*

GALLERIES

As we have seen, fifteenth-century England was a musical country. Even when the dour Reformation came, there was still music in England. In Worcester Cathedral cornets and sackbuts were played at the reception of Queen Elizabeth in 1575. At Canterbury Archbishop Laud appointed two sackbutteers and two corneteers in 1636. P. Smart complained of pipers playing at Durham during the administration of Holy Communion.† It is clear that at first the Reformers had no wish to silence the burst of Church music which enlivened Church services from the quires in the rood lofts, for the object of the Elizabeth's order in 1561 is stated in express terms to be "*for the using or transposing of the rood lofts,*" &c., not at all for their destruction. In another sentence the words occur, "*where in any parish churches the said rood lofts be already transposed.*" Doubtless what was wished was that provision should be made for a gallery for the quire, and that for that purpose the old loft should be taken off the top of the screen and re-erected at the west end of the church in the tower or in front of the tower arch. Many rood lofts were no doubt so shifted or "transposed"; an example remains at Strensham (140). Till quite recently ancient screens were still to be seen in many churches at the west end of the nave. It is extremely unlikely that the parish would have gone to the expense of moving them

* The chief examples remaining are of the fifteenth and sixteenth centuries, viz., Albi Cathedral, La Chaise Dieu, Notre Dame de l'Epine, Brou en Bresse, La Madeleine at Troyes, St Etienne du Mont, Paris, and some beautiful examples in Brittany, *e.g.*, St Fiacre-le-Faouet (85), (Enlart's *Manuel*, 756).

† Walcott's *Traditions of Cathedrals*, 108.

Berkeley Castle Chapel

and preserving them if they were of no use. In most cases they were doubtless used or intended to be used as western galleries. One screen, that at Flamborough (132), has only been removed just recently from the western to the eastern end of the nave. In many cases, probably in the process of removal, their parapets had become insecure, and they were provided with Elizabethan or Jacobean fronts. Great numbers of such

Pyddleton

western galleries existed till they were destroyed by people with no respect for the continuity of the life history of the Church of England. In these western galleries* the villagers did willing and active service to their church. Organs had gone out of

* Fine examples remain at Cullompton, Devon; Pyddleton (Puddle-town), Dorset (1635); Kentisbere, Devon; Newdigate, Surrey (1627); Old Woking, Surrey (1622), and elsewhere. There is a very fine western gallery (181) at Bishop's Cleeve, Gloucester (1640), which the authorities were only stopped from destroying recently by the strong remonstrances of their architect, Mr H. A. Prothero.

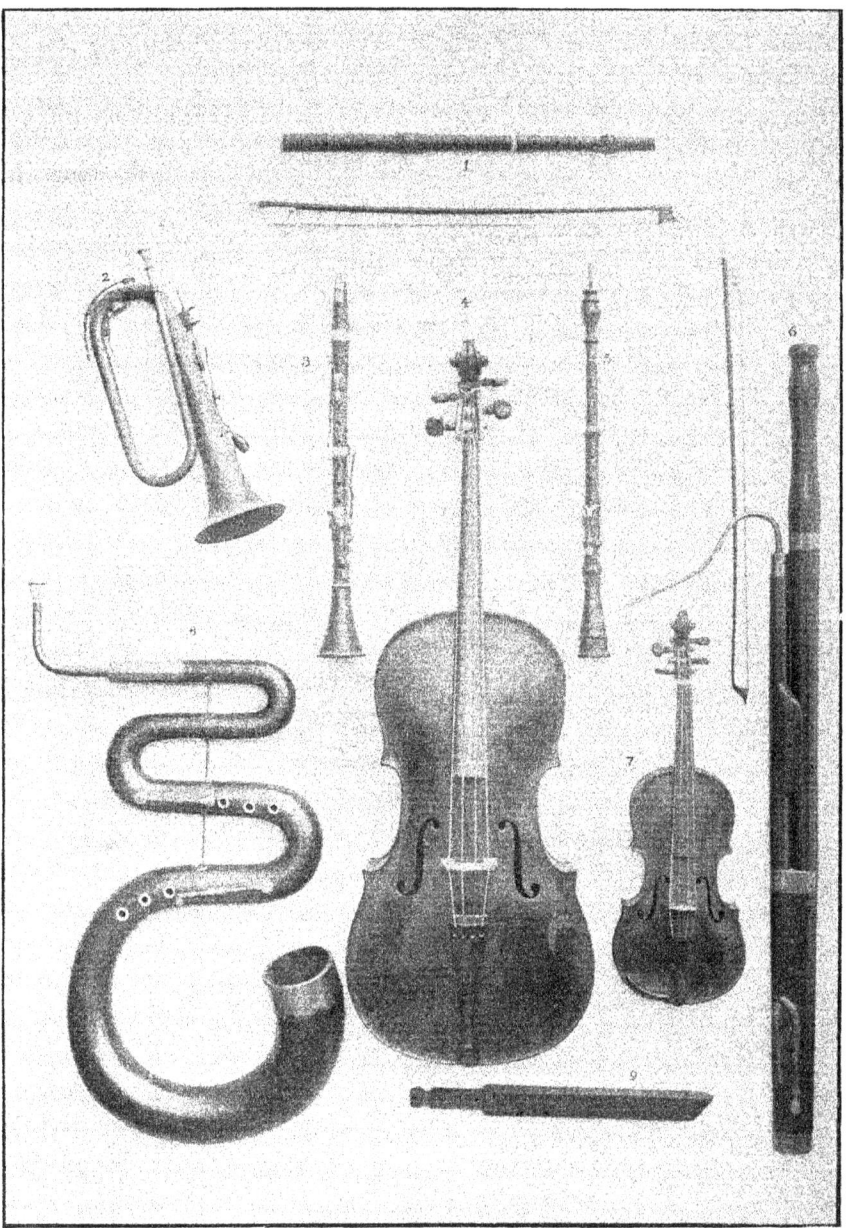

1 Flute
2 Keyed Bugle
3 Clarionet
4 Bass Viol (Violoncello)
5 Hautboy
6 Bassoon
7 Violin
8 Serpent
9 Pitch Pipe

fashion; many villages preferred the parochial church band. The whole array of instruments may still be seen, alas, disused, in some galleries in the West of England, where music lingered long; *e.g.*, at Portishead, Somerset. Some of us have read in Thomas Hardy's *Under the Greenwood Tree* of the happy days before the bands ceased to play in Wessex.* It will surprise many to learn how recently Dorset church bands were to be heard. That at Winterborne Abbas did not disappear till 1881; the last band disappeared in 1895. The church bands are said to have been founded mostly towards the end of the eighteenth century, but the "*true and original Weatherbury Town Band*" had a record of nearly two centuries, and it is hardly likely that for the first of these two centuries it was not in use in church as well as in the town. Mr Galpin thus describes his first introduction to the little church of Winterborne Abbas :—
" Unwonted sounds issued from within, and as we entered the reason became apparent; it was the band getting into tune for their immediate duties. There were three performers; the thatcher (J. Dunford, clerk) played the clarinet and acted as leader, a farm labourer (R. Tompkins) played the flute, while the bass was in the hands of the shepherd (W. Dunford). The absence of the violin was due to the wishes of the parson, who shared the general opinion that it 'savoured of the public-house.' They were placed at the west end of the church under the tower on a rising platform, the violoncello and flute playing at a long desk on the lower steps, while the clarinet stood at a desk on the step above, supported on either side by the singers, and in a position to mark the time for all by the swing of his instrument. ' Let us sing to the praise and glory of God the one hundredth Psalm,' said the rector, whereupon the band struck up in unison (or as near it as the warm afternoon would permit) a curious four-note phrase, which, with various elaborations, was played before each psalm or hymn in the key of the piece following, and was called ' sounding off the tune.' The phrase was evidently based on the old watchmen's refrain, ' Past three o'clock.' Then the singing commenced. For the first verse our trio of musicians arranged itself thus—the clarinet played the air, the flute the tenor (an octave above the voice), and the violoncello the bass. The tune 'going' remarkably well, in the second verse the clarinet proceeded to play the alto an octave higher, so for the remainder of the psalm we were in this order—alto (octave higher), tenor

* See especially the interesting paper by Rev. F. W. Galpin on *Old Church Bands and Village Choirs*, in the *Journal of the Dorset Field Club*, xxvi. 172, from which, with his permission, the following account of Dorset church music is transcribed.

(octave higher), air bass, an arrangement which apparently did not distress the performers or disconcert the singers. At certain places, presumably in sympathy with the words, the clarinet executed original variations. But the church most celebrated in this valley for its instrumental and vocal music was that of Winterborne St Martin or Martinstown. The singers numbered about twenty, with two 'counters' or male-altos, of which the village was justly proud, and in 1820 the band consisted of four clarinets, a hautboy, and a 'base viol,' divided thus — two clarinets for the air, two clarinets for the counter-tenor, the hautboy for the tenor (playing an octave above the voice), and the violoncello for the bass. The hautboy player, a mason, locally known as 'Uncle James,' who also blew 'the loud bassoon' in the village band, was in these early days leader, and gave out the psalms. From a musical standpoint it seems strange that no real tenor instruments were used in any of these bands. At Abbotsbury it is true that there was a 'tenor viol' ('viola'), but apparently it played the alto part. In another village the trombone was in use, but it supported the bass. It seems to have been the general practice to play the tenor part on a treble instrument an octave above the voice, a relic, probably, of the old 'plainsong' days."

The music in Dorset, as well as the musicians, was home made. "John Brown, the carpenter, whose tunes were locally in great request, was choir-master in St Peter's Church, Dorchester, in the early part of the last century. He was evidently not ashamed of his productions, as it was his custom when giving out the number of the psalm, after the privilege of those days, to add 'to a tune of my own composing,' by which well-timed advertisement his fame spread mightily. In the church he divided his performances between playing the fiddle and singing bass, and in the latter capacity he was celebrated for the curious effects he produced by singing through his hands, which he used partly as resonators and partly as a primitive swell. We hear nowadays strong complaints at times against the elaborate setting of the morning and evening canticles to 'services.' But the book of Thomas Richards of Winterborne Abbas, commenced in 1795 and continued through the early years of the next century, shows that in that village church they had 'sarvices' (*sic*) for the Jubilate, Magnificat, and Nunc Dimittis, while the Kyrie Eleison and also the opening Sentences were sung. But in the latter days it is said that the famous Martinstown players were at last reduced to two tunes, vulgarly known at 'thik' or 't'other,' one or other of which had to do duty for all occasions. One of the last exploits of the Winter-

THE VAMPING TRUMPET 147

borne Abbas band was when they attended a wedding at Steepleton, and played out the bride and bridegroom to the suggestive strains of

'Onward, Christian soldiers,
Onward as to *war!*'"

One of the strangest instruments of the old choirs is the vamping trumpet. Five exist: at Braybrook and Harrington, Northants; Willoughton, Lincolnshire; Charing, Kent; and East Leake, Notts The first three are all made in rings or sections, and are all of tin. That at Willoughton is 6 feet long, and the bell has a diameter of 1 foot 4½ inches; that at Braybrook is 5 feet 6 inches long, and the bell has a diameter of 2 feet 1 inch; that at Harrington is 5 feet long, and the bell has a diameter of 1 foot 1 inch; that at Charing is only about 2 feet long. The

East Leake

Braybrook trumpet was in use *c.* 1840. Vamping trumpets do not occur in churchwardens' accounts; but one is mentioned in the *Ishan Diary*, 22, 23. It is there said to have been recently invented by Sir Samuel Morland, and designated the "Stentorophoricum." "Mr Richardson took it to the mill, but we remained near the bowling green, which is a mile off. We could hear distinctly and articulately what Richardson said through the trumpet."* In church they are said to have been used, generally by the leader of the choir, in order to magnify his voice and set the tune of the hymns. Another writer says: "In music the performer of an instrument 'vamps' while the air is played on another. He improvises harmonies to fill up the body of sound and help out the other instruments."

* Miss Florence Peacock in *Reliquary*, 1898, 239.

148 SCREENS AND GALLERIES

Whitby

St Martin's-in-the-Fields

It is interesting to note that a similar transfer of the choir took place in many of the churches of France and Spain in the sixteenth century. At St Nicholas, Troyes, is a fine spacious western gallery in stone of Flamboyant character. A well-known example occurs at Paris. Such galleries, resting on a single segmental stone arch thrown across the western or the two western bays of the nave, are very common in the later Spanish churches, *e.g.*, S. Pablo, Salamanca, and S. Benito, Valladolid.

Just as the rood loft led to the tower gallery and the western gallery, so, on the other hand, it led in many places to an eastern gallery. The transition is well seen in such examples as that of St Mary Magdalen, Taunton, where what had been a rood loft became a private pew. The next step was to build galleries facing west. Usually these were placed on the west of the chancel arch. But sometimes they were constructed to the east of the chancel arch in and above the chancel. Such a chancel gallery was erected in 1635 across the west end of the chancel at East Brent, Somerset. There used to be one over the chancel of Winchcombe, Gloucester, which went by the name of the "Ladies' Gallery." The next step was obvious. With galleries both at the west and the east ends of the nave, why not erect galleries on the north and south sides as well? And erected they were, making a continuous gallery all round. Gallery building began very early. A north gallery was built so early as 1581 in St Leonard, Shoreditch, and there were plenty of galleries by the time of Archbishop Laud, who left an emphatic disapproval of them.* Nowadays they are becoming rare; one may venture to express a hope that not every galleried church may lose the evidence of so interesting a chapter in the long history of the English Church. Few finer specimens are to be found than at Whitby (148) and Monkwearmouth. By Wren and his successors, Hawksmoor and Gibbs, efforts were made, with very considerable success, to make the gallery, constructionally and artistically, an integral part of internal church design. The interiors of St Bride's, Fleet Street; St James's, Piccadilly; and St Martin's-in-the-Fields (148) will repay a visit. From Hawksmoor's fine church of St Mary Woolnoth the galleries were removed, most improperly, in 1876. The west galleries of most of the churches of the above period retain magnificent organs. At times, when a western gallery has gone, proofs of its former presence will be found if looked for. Thus at Shere, Surrey, the external flight of steps to a

* *Hierurgica Anglicana*, ii. 247.

western gallery remains. At St John's, Winchester, is what looks like a blocked clerestory window near the west end of the north wall of the nave. It was once the doorway of a western gallery, reached by an external flight of wooden steps. Frequently also the capitals of the pillars were hacked about in order to make room for the beams of a side gallery; this accounts for such misshapen capitals as those in St Mary, Guildford.

Wenhaston

CHAPTER III

QUIRE SCREENS OF CHURCHES OF SECULAR CANONS

So far we have been speaking mainly of *parish* churches, each with its own parish priest. Sometimes, however, a church had more than one priest. In such a case it was common to incorporate the priests of the church, *i.e.*, they were formed into a corporation or *collegiun*, the priests were called canons, and a church so served is said to be a collegiate church. Collegiate churches are of all sorts and sizes, from a tiny church with but nave and chancel, like Norton, Suffolk, to stately foundations such as Beverley Minster and the cathedrals of the old foundation, all of which are, and always have been, collegiate churches served by secular canons distinguishable from regular canons by the fact that they did not live after a fixed code or rule (*regula*) nor lead a cloistered cœnobitic life, but resided each man in his own house, talking at meals and living at his own sweet will. There is no marked difference between the quire screens of the parish churches and those of the greater collegiate churches and the cathedrals of the old foundation,* except that the latter are on a grander scale, are of solid stone, always had lofts, and were used much more extensively in consequence of the greater elaboration of collegiate and cathedral services. The usual position of the quire screen was the parochial position, viz., at the west end of the quire, under the *eastern* arch of the central tower. There the quire screens still remain at Lincoln, Southwell, Exeter, Wells, Ripon, York—all of stone. At Hereford and St David's the eastern limbs being short, the quire screens stood under the *western* arch of the central tower; the Hereford stalls were only jammed into the eastern limb at a recent "restoration" by Sir Gilbert Scott. At Exeter there is documentary evidence of a couple of altars on the floor of the nave on either side of the

* *I.e.*, Chichester, Exeter, Hereford, Lichfield, Lincoln, London, Salisbury, Wells, York, and the Welsh cathedrals.

152   SCREENS AND GALLERIES

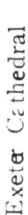

Exeter Cathedral

central doorway of the screen. At Salisbury the epistle, gradual, allelujah, and gospel were sung from the rood loft on all great days; on other days from the quire step.* In all the churches above mentioned the screen may be thought to have been at once quire screen and rood screen, just as in a parish church. But, as we shall see, these two were quite distinct in a monastic church; and though we have little evidence elsewhere for the existence of more than one such screen in churches of secular canons, yet there is one great collegiate church in which undoubtedly, till they were ruthlessly demolished, there were two distinct screens, a stone quire screen to the east and an oak rood screen to the west. This was Ottery St Mary, Devon, as remodelled by Bishop Grandison c. 1337. The two Ottery screens were in exactly the same position as the two in the monastic cathedral of Durham, before they also were "restored" away (166). There was a stone screen in front of the *eastern* arch of the crossing. It was broad and solid, and, till its destruction, the boys of the King's School sat on the top of it. There was a stone staircase inside it, and its west front had a series of niches, which, as at Exeter, were filled with pictures.† The other screen, which was of oak, stood under the *western* arch of the crossing, it had *two* doorways, and the parochial altar used to stand in front of it between them. This open wooden screen, with its two doorways, is standing at this day, in two portions forming parclose screens of the chancel, the doorways now giving access from the quire to its north and south aisles. With this undoubted instance in recent existence it may be that in other churches of secular canons, at any rate in Exeter Cathedral, from which Ottery was copied, documentary or architectural evidence may yet be found proving the existence of separate quire and rood screens.

In most cases the quire screen was of stone, so as to carry a heavy loft and organs, and was solid, in order to secure complete privacy for services in the canons' private chapel, which the quire really was. To build it solid and in stone had, however, a subsidiary advantage, which, where the piers of a central tower threatened to bulge in, *e.g.*, at Ripon, Wells, Darlington, and Canterbury (Benedictine), was of great importance, viz., that it served to shore up the piers on either side. The Arundel screen was removed from the crossing at Chichester

* Frere's *Use of Sarum*, 68-74 and 100-102. At Lichfield there was an altar on the rood loft. Rev. R. M. Serjeantson quotes the following from the Lichfield Episcopal Registers:—"Bishop Scrope founded a chantry, called the Chantry of the Holy Cross, on the rood loft of Lichfield Cathedral."

† Lord Coleridge in *Exeter Dioc. Soc.*, I. iv. 191.

154 SCREENS AND GALLERIES

Howden

York Minster

in 1859, and in the following February *post hoc*, if not *propter hoc*, the central tower and spire collapsed.

The quire screens which survive in cathedrals are those of Lincoln, Southwell,* St David's, Wells, Exeter, Chichester, Ripon, York. Those of Lincoln and Southwell are contemporaneous and sister designs of *c.* 1300. The east side of that of Southwell contains a good deal of beautiful detail in plaster, executed by Bernasconi (169). The Exeter screen was built by Bishop Stapledon between 1317 and 1324. Flanking the central doorway were altars of St Mary and St Nicholas. The work was done by William Canon, and the dean and chapter were so well

St David's

pleased with it that they made him a present of £4 of their courtesy (*ex curialitate*)—about £60 of our money. The screen was solid till side openings were cut through by Sir Gilbert Scott (152). The St David's screen † was built between 1328 and 1347 by Bishop Gower, who is buried in its southern compartment. In the northern compartment is a reredos, in front of which there was originally a side altar (155). The Wells screen seems to belong to the second quarter of the fourteenth century. It was consider-

* There is a measured drawing of the Lincoln screen by Mr John Begg in the *Architectural Association Sketch Book*, 3, i. 46; and of the Ripon screen in the *Architectural Association Sketch Book*, x. 6.

† Measured drawings in the *Spring Gardens Sketch Book*, v. 30 and 31.

ably altered by Mr Salvin at a restoration, which was bad enough as it was, but which would have been still more disastrous if Professor Freeman's evil suggestion had been adopted, to remove the screen altogether in order to fit the cathedral for parochial use. The screens of York and Ripon are sister designs, both executed *c.* 1490 and both in the same diocese. Both contain a big central doorway surmounted by an ogee hood-mold, and flanked by niches to hold statues. Those of York represent the Kings of England from William the Conqueror to Henry VI., and are original, except that of Henry VI., which may have been removed because there was a tendency everywhere to venerate him as a saint. The figures of angels above the canopies in the niches are in plaster by Bernasconi, who also executed certain other restorations (154). The Chichester screen is attributed to Bishop Arundel (1459-1478). It stood under the western arch of the central tower. It has been set up again quite recently, much modernised.

It is not possible to describe separately the many notable screens of the collegiate churches. At Howden, under the western arch of the central tower, is a stone screen which Mr Petit * calls a rood screen, but it is plainly a quire screen, for it has a central doorway. This doorway is roofed with a depressed barrel vault, evidently of late date (154).

* *Arch. Journal*, xxv. 179.

CHAPTER IV

SCREENS IN CHURCHES OF MONKS AND REGULAR CANONS

THE arrangements of the churches of the Austin and Premonstratensian canons may be discussed together with those of the Benedictine, Cluniac, and Cistercian monks, for all the "regulars," whether monks or canons, lived the "common" life in a cloister, the chief difference being that all the canons were priests. Their arrangements were quite different from those of parish churches. It is largely from ignorance of or indifference to this fact that so much confusion has been introduced into the history of English church screens; what was true only of monastic screens being assumed to be true also of collegiate and parochial ones. Even when it is recognised that there was not one but at least two distinct screens—one the pulpitum or quire screen, the other the rood screen—in a church of monks or regular canons, the two are constantly confounded. Thus, the architect who conducted the restoration of Christchurch, Hants, wrote a paper on the screen still in existence there, under the title of *The Rood Screen of Christchurch.* It is not a rood screen at all, but stands under the *eastern* arch of the crossing, and is a quire screen, with a single central doorway (158). Moreover, he noted that the first piers west of the crossing lack the projecting semicircular roof-shafts of the rest of the piers of the nave. He did not draw the conclusion that it was just between these piers that the real rood screen stood originally. His mistake about the pulpitum was excusable enough, for the reverse mistake was made by the monk Gervase, who says that at Canterbury Cathedral before the fire of 1174 there was a *pulpitum* which separated the central tower from the nave, and had in the middle and on the side towards the nave the altar of the Holy Cross.* Really this was not at all what is nowadays

---

* Willis' *Canterbury Cathedral*, 37.

Christchurch

called a "pulpitum." It stood under the western arch of the crossing, and had a central altar west of it, and therefore two lateral doorways, and was a rood screen. Again at St Margaret's, Westminster, which is neither a monastic nor a collegiate church, there is an item in the accounts of 1560 "for new organs in the *pulpitte."* But this is neither a pulpitum nor a rood screen, but a parochial chancel screen. The quire screen at Exeter is also called a pulpitum in the accounts. Evidently the term "pulpitum" was used in a loose sort of way of the *loft*, whatever kind of screen it surmounted.

THE QUIRE SCREEN OR PULPITUM

In order to avoid such confusion, it may be suggested that in future, where there are two screens, the terms *pulpitum* and *quire screen* should be confined to the eastern and the term *rood screen* to the western of the two; while, when pulpitum and rood screen are blended in one, as in a parish church, it should be spoken of as a *chancel screen.* The pulpitum differed from the rood screen in many ways. It formed the eastern barrier of the quire, and against the eastern face of it were placed the return stalls, *i.e.,* those facing east, of the greater officials of the house. It was much broader than the rood screen, often occupying, when placed in the nave, a whole bay, *e.g.,* at Norwich (166), while the rood screen was often merely a wall between two piers; it is described as a wall in the *Rites of Durham.* At St Albans, however, the rood screen, which still exists, is more roomy, and has a loft above it (162). The pulpitum always had a spacious loft above it, and carried the organ. Down below it there was a single central passage through into the quire. On its western face there was a side altar on either side of the central doorway. In Pugin's time the remains of these side altars could still be seen at Norwich. They have been removed, and modern work has been put in their place. The loft was reached by one or two staircases. The position of the pulpitum was determined by the respective lengths of the eastern and western limbs of the church. If the nave was long, as at Ely, Peterborough, Bayham, and Westminster, there was room in its western bays for the stalls of the monks and canons. Even if it was not very long, the stalls had to be placed in it, if the eastern limb was too short to serve as more than sacrarium or presbytery, as at Furness and Dore. Sometimes the eastern limb was greatly lengthened at a later period, and in such cases the screens might be rebuilt on a different site. This seems to be the case at Dunstable, where the screen has now two side doors, and is therefore a rood screen. But, since there is a blocked door in the centre of it, it is probably the ancient pulpitum converted into a rood screen at the time of great eastern extensions. Of these pulpita or quire screens several still survive *in situ*, *e.g.*, in the Benedictine churches of Canterbury, Rochester, Malmesbury, Norwich, and in the Austin Canons' churches of Carlisle, Christchurch, Hexham, and Bolton, and the Cistercian church of Melrose.* Of the monastic pulpita, that of Canterbury was erected by Prior Chillenden, *c.* 1400; both its masonry and most of its statues survive almost unaltered. The Norwich pulpitum was built by Bishop Lyhart between 1446 and 1472; only the lower part is original (166). The Rochester pulpitum is entirely covered on its western face with modern carving and statuary; but on its eastern side is the original wooden screen of 1227, probably the very earliest screen now existing in England. At Malmesbury the ancient pulpitum is incorporated with the wall with which the east end of the nave was built up, when the church lost its quire and transepts at the Dissolution. It has a central doorway, and its cornice contains the arms and badges of Henry VI. At Christchurch, Hants, the pulpitum is of stone, and has a central doorway, and some of its niches retain exquisite undulatory foliage of oak, hazel, acorns, nuts, &c., whose naturalistic character shows that the work belongs to the first quarter of the fourteenth century (158). At Hexham a fine wooden pulpitum survives, with its loft.†

* The situation of the pulpitum varied considerably. Where the stalls were wholly in the eastern limb, it was placed under the *eastern* arch of the crossing, *e.g.*, in the cathedrals of Canterbury, Rochester, Durham, and Milton Abbas (Benedictine), at Bristol, Carlisle, Hexham, and Christchurch, Hants (Augustinian Canons). It occupied the westernmost bay of the nave at Winchester, Gloucester, Malmesbury (Benedictine); Valle Crucis, Beaulieu, Buildwas (Cistercian). It occupied the second bay from the east in the Cistercian naves of Tintern and Fountains, and in the long Benedictine naves of Peterborough and Ely. Brown-Willis shows it on his plan of Ely as the western barrier of the choir stalls which extended across and west of of the octagon till the "restoration" and disturbance of 1757, and describes it as the "stone gallery where the organ stands." But on his plan he gives it three doorways or openings of some sort. There is said to be a sketch of it in the British Museum, but it is mislaid. It occupied the third bay in Benedictine Norwich, and in the Cistercian naves of Waverley, Furness, Dore, and Roche. In Benedictine Westminster it occupied the fourth bay, as may be seen to this day.

† Illustrated in Hodges' *Hexham Abbey*.

The Rood Screen

The rood screen was normally a solid wall with a little doorway on either side; sometimes, as at St Albans, it was more roomy (162). Above it was a loft. Above the loft was the great Rood and the Mary and John. Between the side doorways was a central altar. In the Cistercian churches this altar was the altar of the lay brothers or *fratres conversi*, till these were abolished; in the Benedictine and Augustinian churches it was the parochial altar of the laity in general. It was sometimes called the Jesus altar, sometimes the Holy Cross * altar, in reference to the great rood above. Towards the end of the great Sunday procession, when all the rest of the church had been perambulated, as well as the cloister and its surrounding buildings, the monks or canons entered the nave by the western of the two doorways leading from the cloister, and marching up the nave in double file took their stand on the double row of processional stones laid for that purpose down the centre of the nave, and there made their principal "station" before the Jesus altar. Then they passed in *two* files through the two doorways of the rood screen, when the procession formed in *double* file and passed through the single central doorway of the pulpitum, and then, filing to the right and left into their stalls, commenced High Mass. The Durham rood screen is described at length in the *Rites*, page 28. It occupied the easternmost bay of the nave. "In the body of the church, between two of the highest pillars supporting . . . the west side of the Lantern tower   there was an altar called *Jesus' Altar*, where Jesus' Mass was sung every Friday throughout the whole year. And behind the said altar was a fair high stone wall (the *rood screen*). At either end of the wall there was a door, which was locked every night, called the *two rood doors*, for the procession to go forth and come in at, and between those two doors was Jesus' Altar placed." On the face of this rood screen was depicted in stone the story and Passion of our Lord; above, that of the twelve Apostles; and above that was a cornice "very artificially wrought in stone, with marvellous fine colours, very curiously and excellently finely gilt with branches and flowers, the more that a man did look on it, the more was his affection to behold it." Above the rood screen was the rood. "Above the height of all did stand the most goodly and famous rood that was in this land, with the picture of Mary on the one side and the picture of John on the

---

* At Norwich it became in later days the altar of St William.

162   SCREENS AND GALLERIES

St Albans

other, with two splendent and glistering Archangels, one on the one side of Mary, and the other of the other side of John. So what for the fairness of the rood screen, the stateliness of the pictures, and the livelihood of the painting, it was thought to be one of the goodliest monuments in that church." The arrangement of the screens in the Cistercian Abbey of Fountains is shown clearly in Mr W. H. St John Hope's plan. The monks' quire occupied the whole of the crossing and the first bay of the nave. The second bay was wholly filled with the *pulpitum*, through which ran a central passage. In the third bay there were probably two altars, as at Furness, Roche, and Revesby, one on each side of the central doorway of the pulpitum. The fourth bay was free. Between the pillars which formed the western boundary of this fourth bay was the *rood screen*. This had *two* doorways. The fifth bay was occupied by the Jesus or Rood or Holy Cross altar.*

Only one rood screen is left to us complete, that of St Albans, and unfortunately the pulpitum at St Albans is gone, so that we cannot see now anywhere in England the spectacle of both pulpitum and rood screen. But any one with a little imagination can realise what the combination looks like if he conceives of the rood screen at St Albans planted in Norwich Cathedral nave two bays west of the present pulpitum (the exact site is marked in the plan on page 166); or if he imagines the pulpitum at Canterbury set one or two bays east of the rood screen of St Albans. Otherwise, he may go to the Cistercian abbey of Maulbronn in Wurtemberg, where he will find both pulpitum and rood screen *in situ*, the pulpitum occupying the fourth bay from the central tower, and the rood screen wall placed between the two eastern piers of the sixth bay (166). But for the vandals of Ottery St Mary we could have seen all this at home. But though we have but one rood screen *in situ* in the middle of a church, viz., at St Albans, we have by a curious accident several rood screens now forming the *eastern walls* of their churches. In all these cases these are churches of the Regulars in which the quire and the transepts have been destroyed, and sometimes a bay or two of the nave next to the crossing. Visit the churches of Blyth and Crowland (Benedictine), or Dunstable, Waltham, Bolton, Newark (Augustinian), and it will be found that the nave terminates to the east in a wall containing two doorways, now objectless and blocked up, between which is or was the nave altar. That altar is and always has been the parochial altar; the nave west of it is and

---

* Hope, *Fountains*, 39.

always has been parochial. When the suppression of 1538 came, the parishioners of these churches very properly refused to let their parochial part of the church be confiscated, and so the present parish church is the identical parochial nave of the old Benedictine or Augustinian church. Such continuity is there in the history of our ancient English Church! At Boxgrove the case is different (164). Here the parish apparently got a grant of the Benedictine quire and transept, and let the parochial nave

Boxgrove

go to ruin so that the present parish church is the ancient monastic quire.* A similar arrangement existed at Ewenny and Brecon priories.

* The rood screen occupied the western arch of the crossing at Durham and Croyland (Benedictine), and at Bolton and Waltham (Augustinian). It was placed between the first piers from the crossing at Dunstable, Newark, Surrey, and Christchurch, Hants (Augustinian). It was between the second piers from the crossing at Tewkesbury, Gloucester, and Boxgrove (Benedictine). It was between the third piers at St Albans and Winchester (Benedictine). It was between the fourth piers at Fountains (Cistercian) and Bayham (Premonstratensian). It was between the fifth piers at Norwich (Benedictine) and Dore (Cistercian).

Fence Screens

Usually, probably, the chief altars were protected by wooden screens of openwork placed in front of them. That of Dunstable remains, *i.e.*, there is a wooden screen in front of the altar as well as a stone rood screen behind it. At Maulbronn also all three survive, viz., pulpitum, rood screen, and fence screen (166). In the Cistercian abbey of Buildwas there seems to have been a fence screen crossing the nave west of the rood screen.* In Norwich nave it may be seen that the next pier west of the existing pulpitum on each side has its pair of vaulting shafts stopped short at corbels. These corbels show exactly how high the three screens of each of the side altars rose. The plan of Gloucester nave in Brown Willis shows that there also the side altars of the pulpitum were fenced in by screens.† The *Rites of Durham*, page 28, speak of a fence screen as in front of the nave altar there. "The height of it was something above a man's breast, and in the height of the said door it was all stricken full of iron piks, that no man should climb over." Mr F. Bligh Bond notes that in some instances in parish churches also, as at Guilden Morden, Cambridge, the altars beneath the quire screen were entirely enclosed by "cancelli" of light traceried screenwork.‡

* See plan by Mr Roland W. Paul in *Builder*, 6th October 1900.
† Such "fence screens" are, strictly speaking, "parclose screens," but it is convenient to have a special term in a church of the "Regulars" for screenwork in front of a high altar, or the two altars in front of a pulpitum, or the one altar in front of a rood screen.
‡ In the plans of Norwich Cathedral and Maulbronn Abbey (166), A denotes the quire screen or pulpitum, B the rood screen, C a fence screen. In the plan of Ottery St Mary, 1 is the screen of the Lady Chapel, 2 is the high reredos of the high altar (the upper part of the back of which is seen on page 37), 3 is the quire screen or pulpitum, 4 the rood screen.

166 SCREENS AND GALLERIES

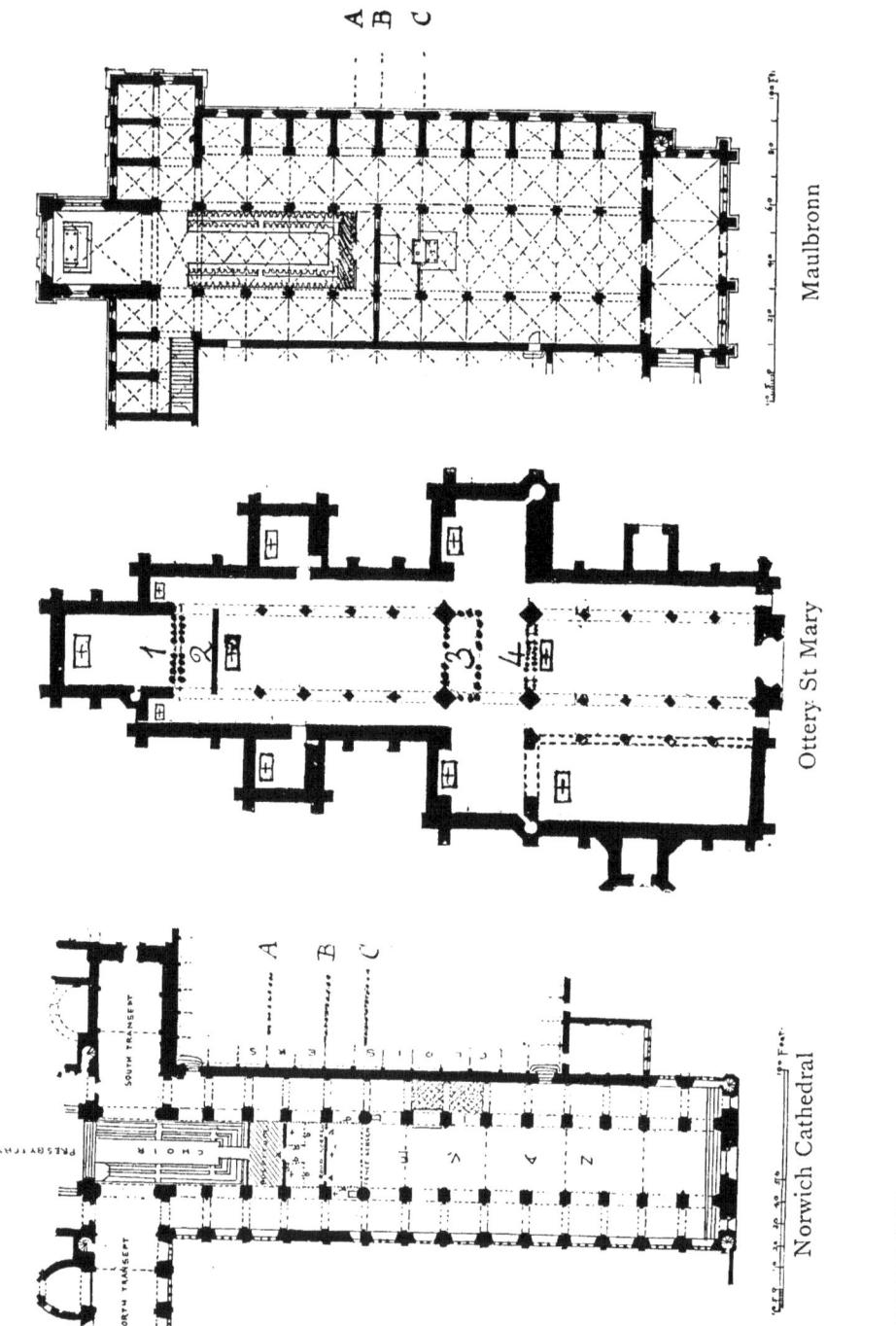

Maulbronn

Ottery St Mary

Norwich Cathedral

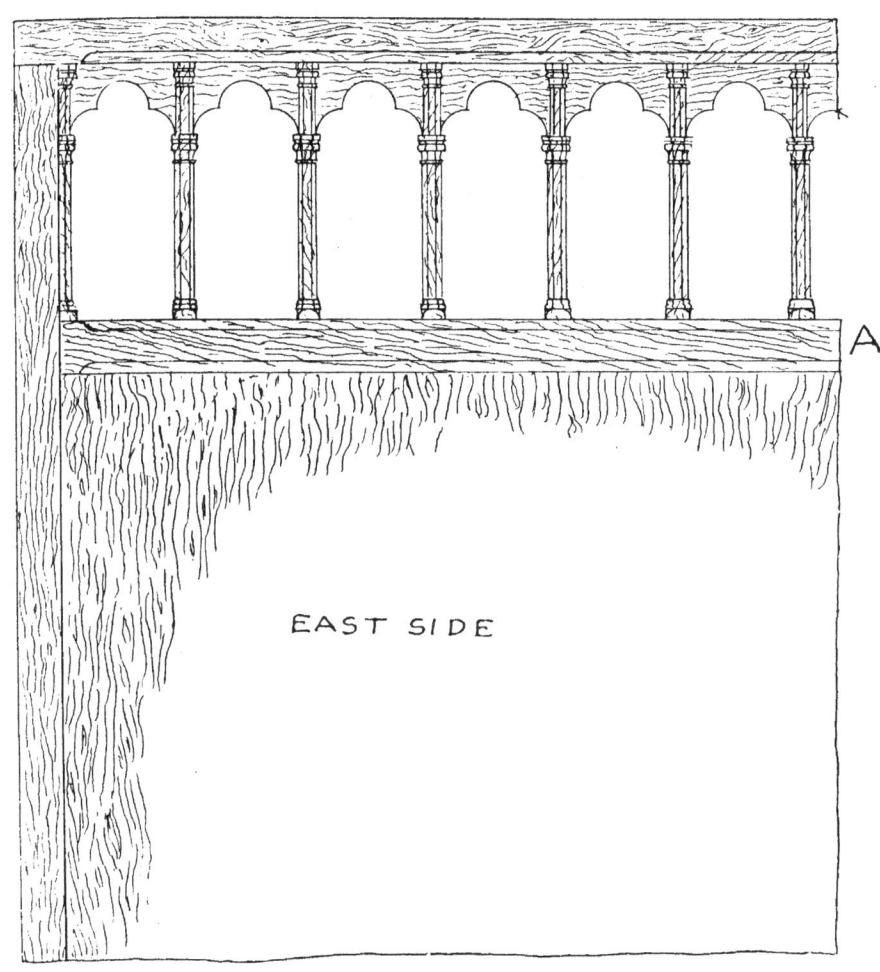

Rochester

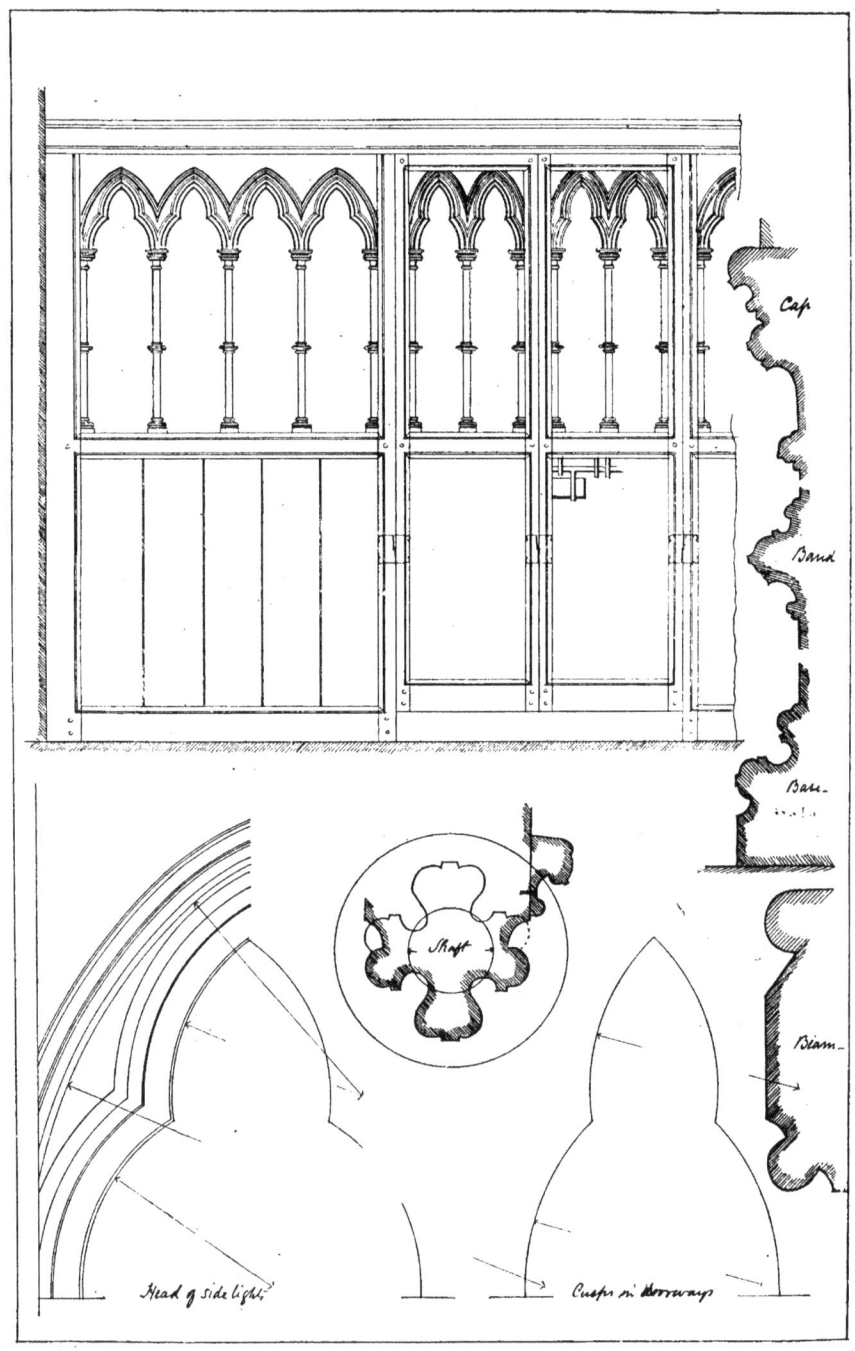

Stanton Harcourt

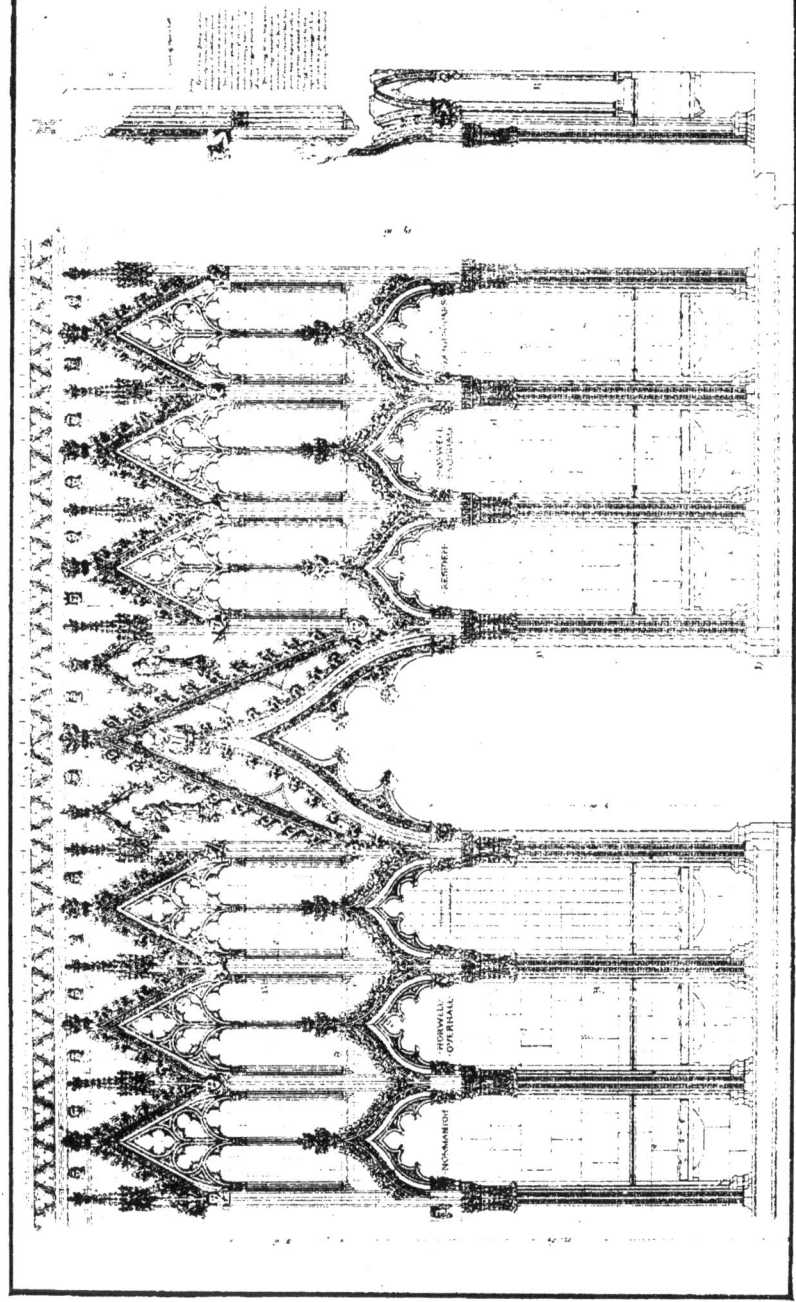

Southwell

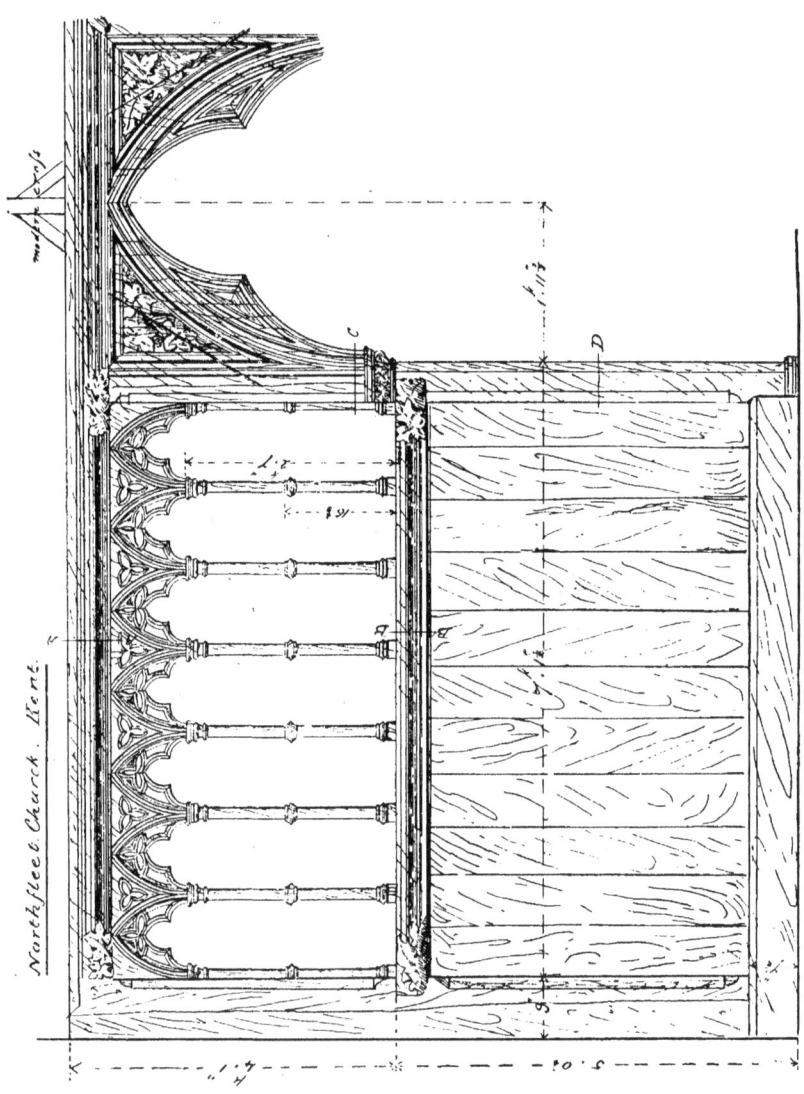

MEASURED DRAWINGS

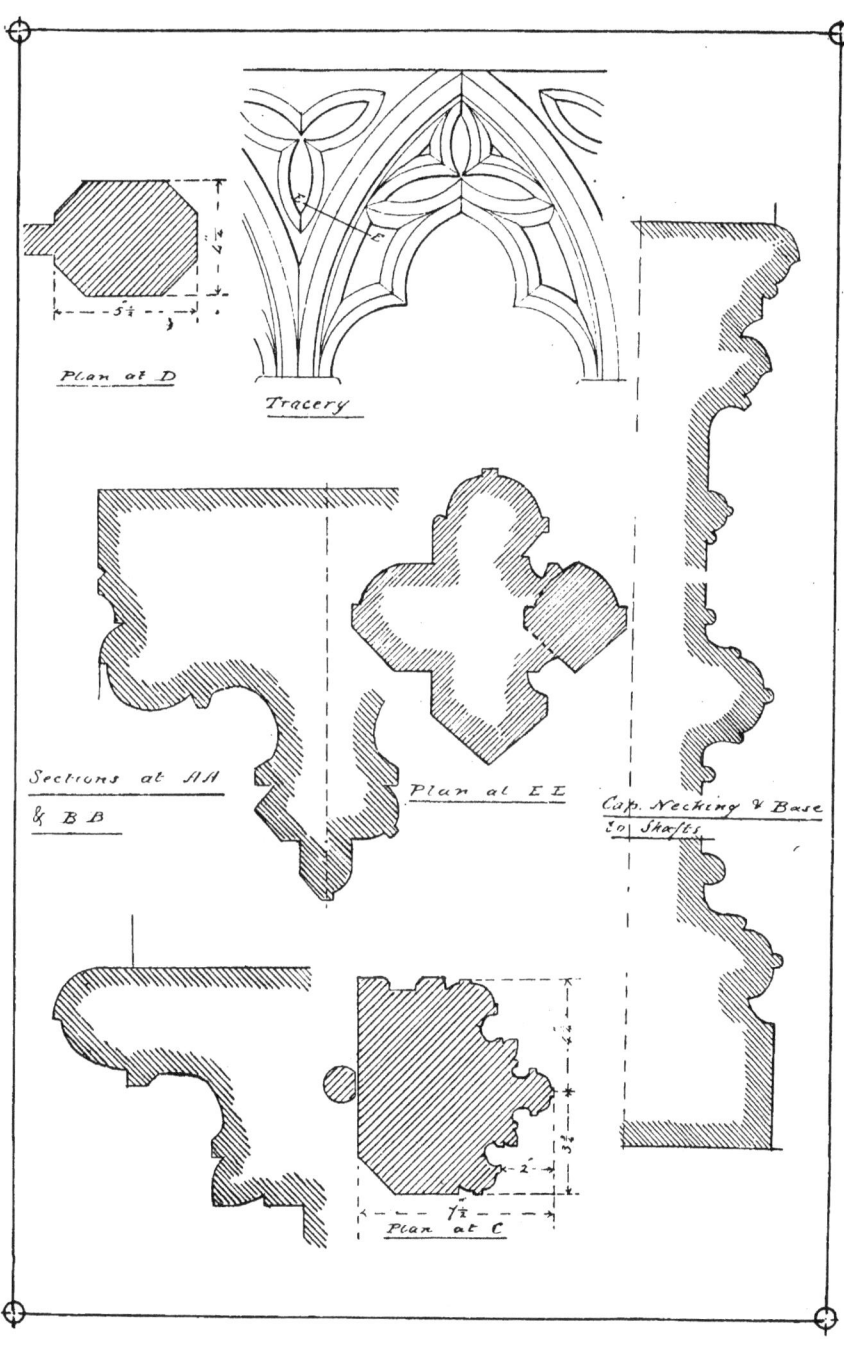

Northfleet

Watlington

MEASURED DRAWINGS

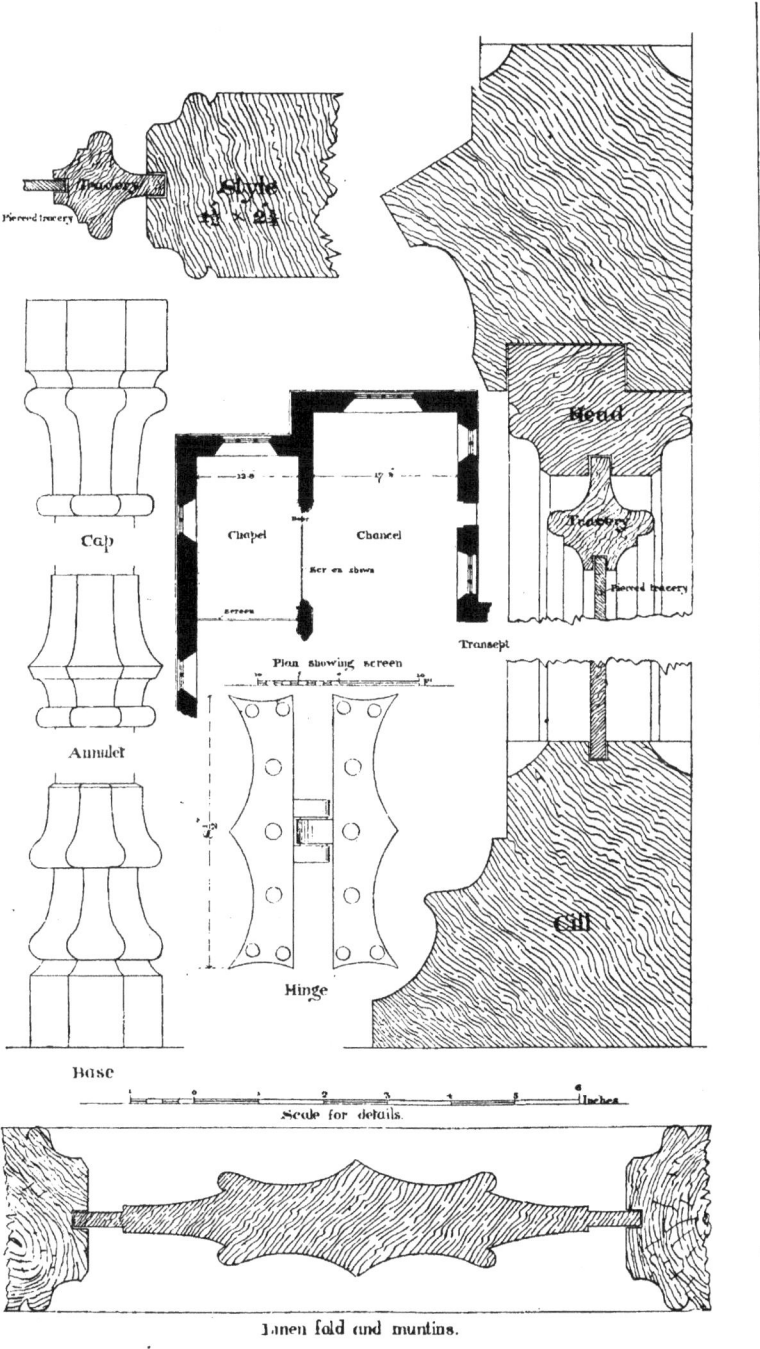

Colebrook (see Photograph on p. 84)

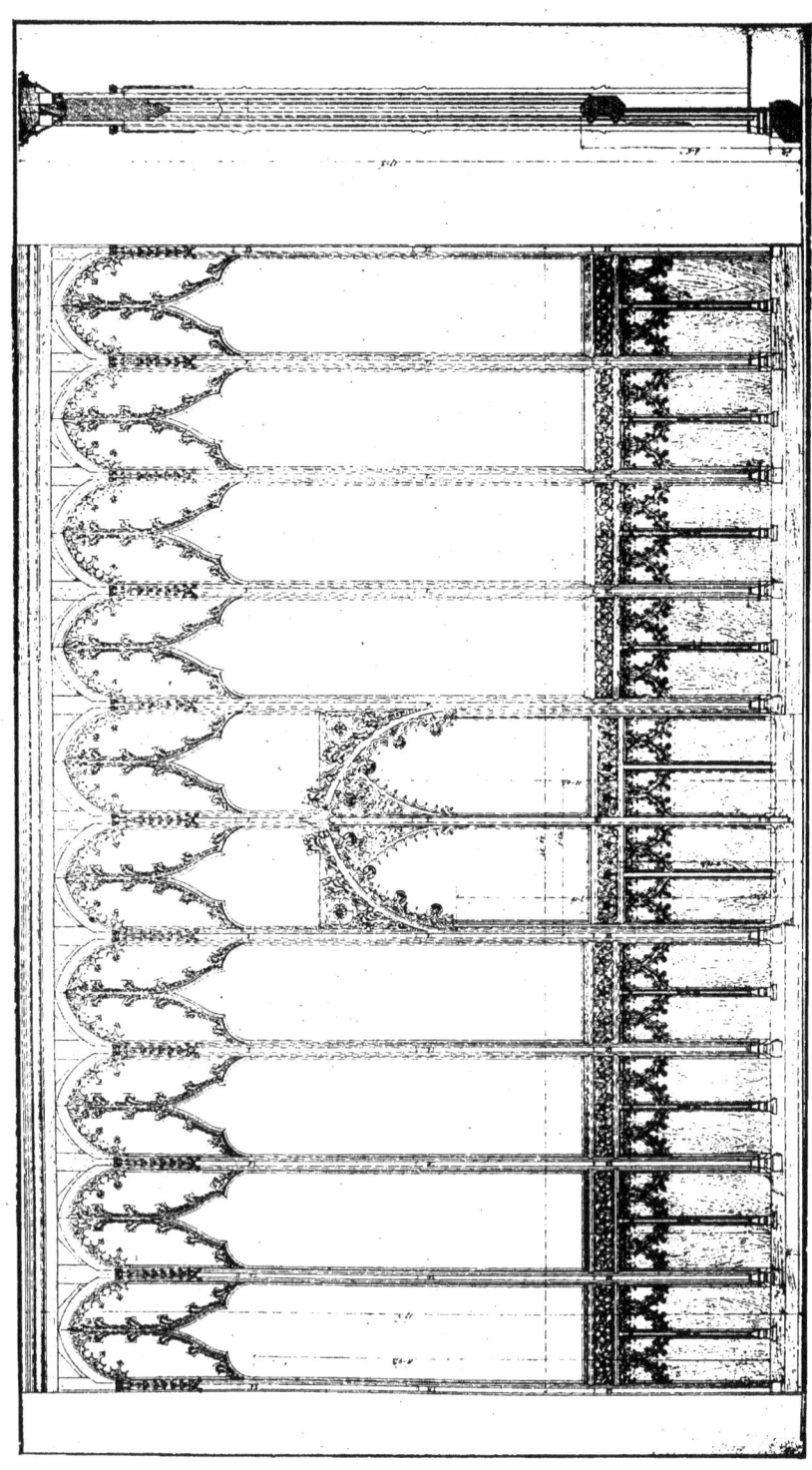

Cawston

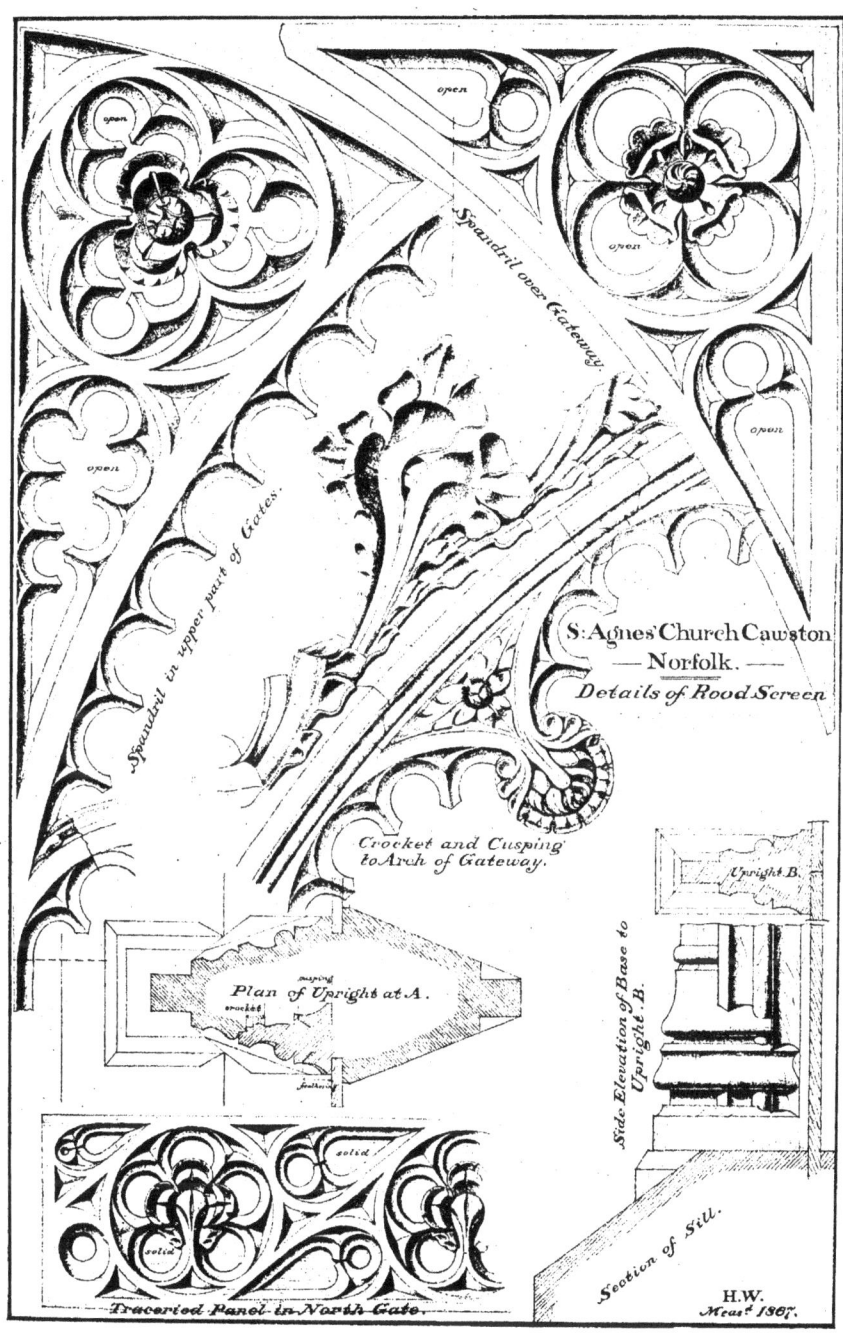

Acle

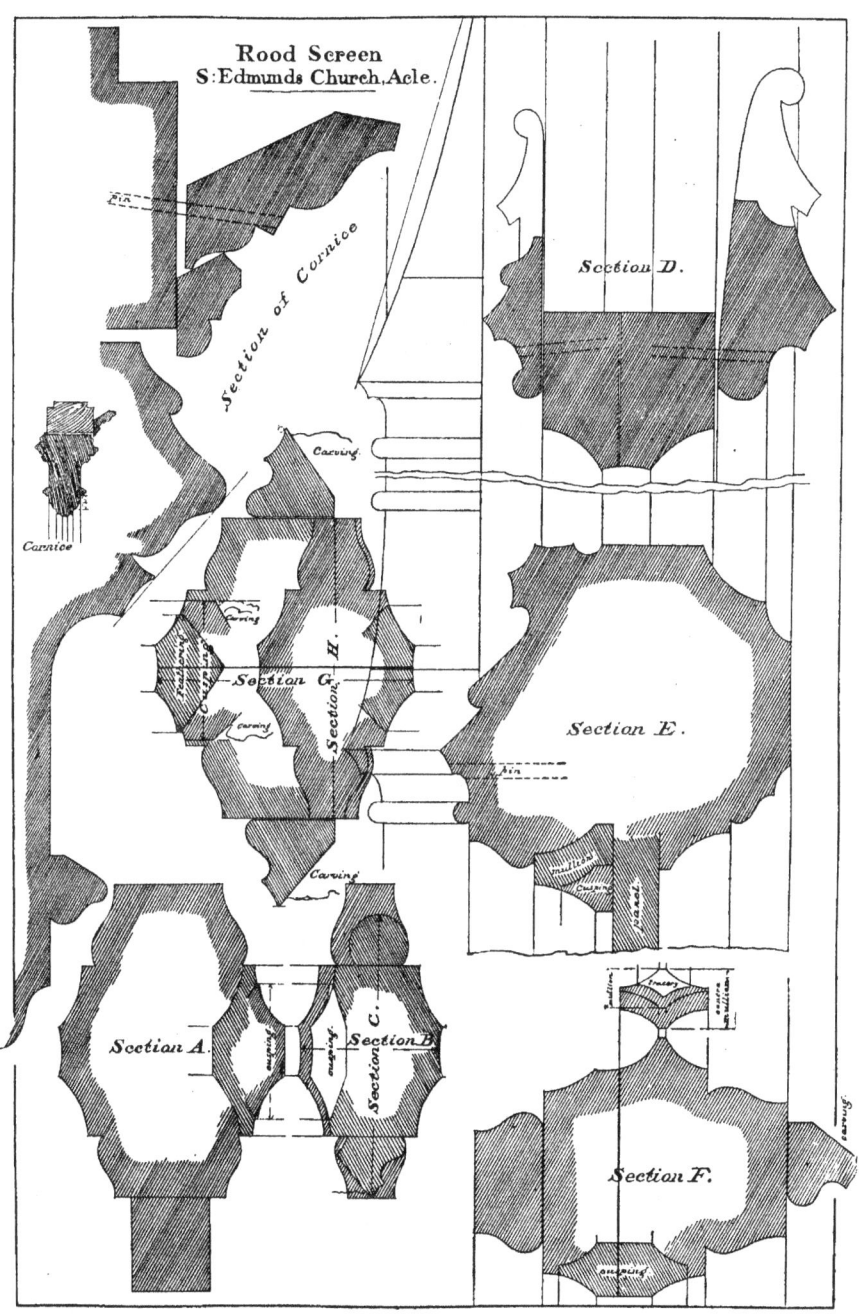

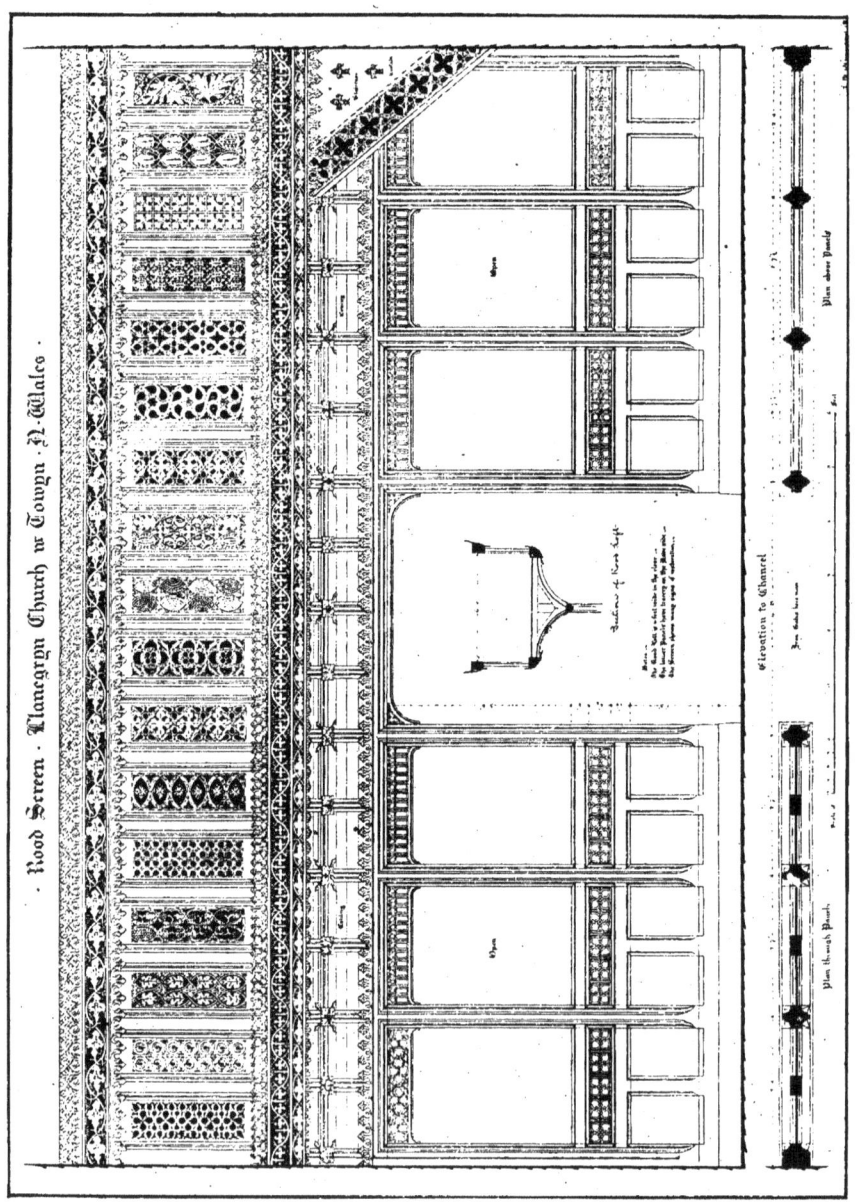

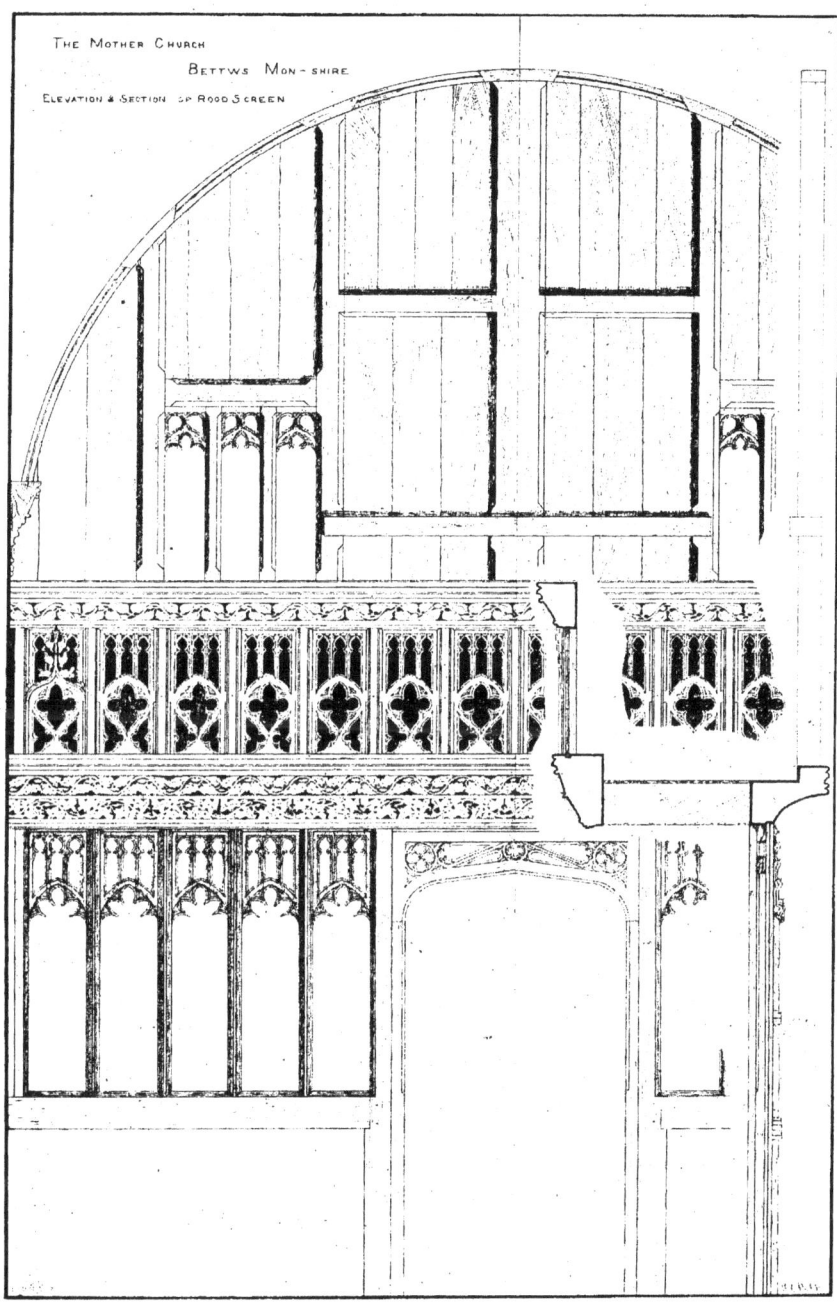

Bettws Newydd

SCREENS AND GALLERIES

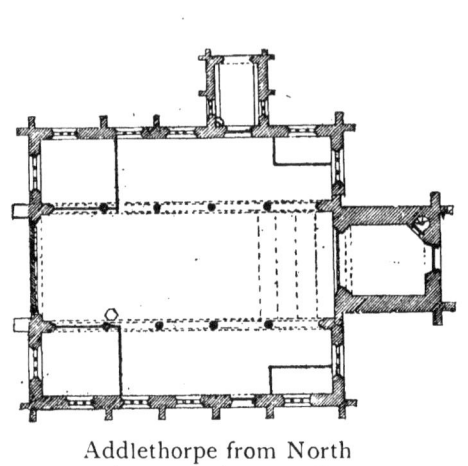

Addlethorpe from North
(Chancel destroyed)

Addlethorpe

Bishop's Cleeve

INDEX LOCORUM

Place.	Text.	Illustration.	Source.
Acle		176	Norman Taylor.
Do. (detail)		177	do.
Addlethorpe		180	H. Vaughan.
Do. (plan)		180	do.
Albi		...	
Ashburton		...	...
Astbury		19	G. G. Buckley.
Atherington	42, 117	43	F. H. Crossley.
Aylmerton		...	
Aylsham		...	
Baginton		...	
Band (Church)		144	F. W. Galpin.
Banwell		...	
Barningham		53	F. Bond.
Barton Turf		...	
Baulking		...	
Bengeworth		...	
Benniworth		...	...
Berkeley		142	Oscar Clark in *Bristol and Gloucester Arch. Journal*.
Bettws Newydd	86, 125	179	H. A. Prothero.
Bettys-Gwerfil-Goch	101	...	
Binsted	107	...	...
Bishop's Cleeve	143	181	Messrs Phillott and Barnard.
Do.		181	do.
Do.		181	do.
Bletchingley		...	...
Blewbury		116	W. Marshall.
Blundeston		54	F. Bond.
Blyth		...	
Bolton Priory		...	...
Bottisham		25	G. H. Tyndall.
Bovey Tracey		62	F. H. Crossley.
Do. (detail)		63	do.
Boxgrove		164	Amy Chown.
Bradford Abbas		26	H. Bedford Pim.

Place.	Text.	Illustration.	Source.
Bradwell	125	126	A. B. Bamford in *Essex Arch. Trans.*
Do., St Peter on the Wall	7	...	
Bramfield	49, 75	76	F. Bond.
Bramford	8, 24, 38	24	A. W. Payne.
Brecon	17, 164	...	...
Bridford	38, 60, 66, 98, 111, 139	138	F. H. Crossley.
Brightlingsea	136	...	
Brilley	17	...	
Brimpton	26	...	
Bristol Cathedral	133, 135	...	
Do., St Mary Redcliffe	115	...	...
Brixworth	7	...	
Broadwater	107	102	F. Bond.
Brushford	87	...	
Buildwas	165	...	
Burlingham	75	...	
Bury St Edmund	8, 103	...	
Cambridge, Great St Mary		...	
Do. King's		91	F. Bond.
Canterbury Cathedral	4,		
Do., St Alphege			
Do., St Dunstan			
Do., St Pancras			...
Capel-le-Ferne		23	H. Bedford Pim.
Carlisle			...
Cartmel		90	H. E. Illingworth.
Do.		90	do.
Castle Rising			
Cawston (screen)		174	H. Walker.
Do. (detail)		175	do.
Do. (two saints)		74	W. Davidson.
Charlton on-Otmoor		102	J. F. East.
Chedzoy		...	
Chichester		...	
Chipping Norton		...	
Christchurch		158	H. E. Miller.
Do. (detail)		158	do.
Do. do.		158	do.
Church Handborough		112	J. F. East.
Cirencester		...	
Cliffe		...	
Colchester		..	
Colebrook		84	F. H. Crossley.
Do. (detail)		173	A. Langdon.
Coleridge		...	
Coltersworth		...	
Colyton		34	E. K. Prideaux.

INDEX LOCORUM

Place.	Text.	Illustration.	Source.
Compton		...	
Do. Bassett		35	Miss Ransome.
Congresbury		64	F. H. Crossley
Constantinople		...	...
Cotes-by-Stow		120	H. Bedford Pim.
Covehithe		114	F. Bond.
Credenhill		...	...
Croscombe		95	W. Marshall.
Crowcombe			
Crowland		...	
Cruwys Morchard		...	...
Cullompton		104	W. Marshall.
Darlington	153	...	
Dauntsey	129	...	
Dennington (interior)	15, 24, 115	14	F. Bond.
Do. (screen)	24, 49	14	do.
Derwen	77	...	
Dunchideock	66, 117	118	F. H. Crossley.
Dunster	17, 119	16	F. J. Allen in *Somerset Arch. Journal.*
Dunstable	150, 163, 165	...	
Durham	99, 141, 161	...	
Eartham	24	27	H. Bedford Pim.
East Brent	149	...	
East Harling	22, 49	22	F. Bond.
East Leake	147	147	E. L. Guilford.
Edington	105, 113	...	
Elworthy	42	...	
Ely	160	...	
Erith	117	...	
Ewenny	164	...	
Exeter (quire screen)	107, 151, 155, 159	152	M. P. Perry.
Do., St Mary Magdalen	22	35	E. K. Prideaux.
Flamborough	113, 133, 143	132	C. Goulding.
Fountains	163	...	
Fritton	93	92	F. Bond.
Gateley	75		
Gillingham	75		
Gloucester	165		
Grantham	122		
Greywell	113		
Great Bardfield	8, 32, 107	29	H. T. Lawson.
Guilden Morden	42, 165		
Guildford, St Mary	150		
Hadleigh	56	52	G. G. Buckley.
Harberton	13, 66, 117	12	F. H. Crossley.
Do.	135	134	do.

Place.	Text.	Illustration.	Source.
Harlestone	136	...	
Hartland	117	...	
Hauxton	10	...	
Hawton	94	...	
Headbourne Worthy	103	...	
Heckington	136	...	
Hereford	151	...	
Hexham	160	...	...
High Ham	48, 66, 111	65	F. H. Crossley.
Highway	28	...	...
Hitchin	56	58	A. Whitford Anderson
Holbeton	59, 60	Frontispiece	F. H. Crossley.
Do. (detail)	66, 87	89	do.
Hoo	125	...	...
Horning	123	...	
Howden	156	154	F. Bond.
Hubberholme	115, 125	...	
Kenton	59, 60, 119	106	F. H. Crossley.
Do. (detail)	48, 66, 87	88	do.
Kirkstead	87	...	...
Knapton	105	...	...
Lapford	103	100	F. H. Crossley.
Lastingham	125	...	...
Lavenham (chancel screen)	56	51	G. G. Buckley.
Do. (parclose)	21, 22	19	do.
Leeds, St John	99	...	...
Lew Trenchard	66, 119	...	
Lichfield	153	...	
Lincoln	151, 155	...	
Littleham	70	...	
Little Hereford	122	...	
Little Malvern	105	...	
Llananno	77	80	A. Watkins.
Do. (detail)	86	81	do.
Llandinabo	87	...	..
Llanegryn	77, 86, 111	178	E. B. Nevinson.
Llangwm	10	...	
Llanwnog	77	...	...
Llanrwst, W.	77, 101, 111	82	A. Watkins.
Do., E.	86, 105, 119	83	do.
London, St Margaret's, Lothbury	99	...	
Do., St Martin-in-the-Fields	149	148	E. W. M. Wonnacott.
Do., St Mary Woolnoth	149	...	
Do., St Paul's	141	...	
Do., St Peter Cheap	103	..	
Do., St Peter's, Cornhill	99	...	

Place.	Text.	Illustration.	Source.
London, St Stephen Walbrook -			
Long Aston - -			
Long Melford -			
Louth -			
Low Ham -			
Ludham -			
Lullingstone -			
Lullington - -			
Luton - -			
Lyminge - -			
Lynsted - -			
Malmesbury -		...	
Manchester -		...	
Marsham -		...	
Marwood -		67	F. H. Crossley.
Maulbronn -		166	R.I.B.A. *Journal.*
Maxey - -		122	J. F. East.
Melton Constable -		7	H. Bedford Pim.
Melton Mowbray -		...	
Merrington -		...	
Michaelchurch - -		...	
Milborne, Dorset -		...	
Milborne Port - -		113	E. W. M. Wonnacott.
Minehead - - -		69	G. W. Saunders.
Mobberley -		44	Mrs Jessie Lloyd.
Do. (detail) -		45	do.
Mochre -			
Montgomery -			
Monza -			
Nantwich - -	121		
Newark Abbey - -	163		
Newark Church -	119		
Newport - - -	77		
Northenden -	42		
Northfleet - -	93	170	H. T. Keates in *Arch. Assoc. Sketch Book.*
Do. (detail) -	93	171	
North Walsham - -	15, 139	...	
Norwich (plan) - -	159, 160, 161, 165	166	Walcott.
Do., St John Timberhill -	125	...	
Ottery (screen) -	22, 24	37	W. Marshall.
Do. (plan) -	153, 165	166	*Exeter Diocesan Soc. Journal.*
Old Shoreham -	107		
Ovingdean -	7		
Paignton - -	34, 38	...	
Patricio - -	10, 28, 27	78	A. Watkins.
Do. (detail) - -	86	79	do.

Place.	Text.	Illustration.	Source.
Peterchurch	10	...	
Portishead	145	...	...
Postling	17		
Priziac	119		
Probus	42	...	
Puxley	87	...	
Pyddleton	143	143	F. R. Taylor.
Pyecombe	7	...	
Ranworth	11, 68, 70, 73, 77		
Do. (St George)	70	71	W. Davidson.
Do. (St Michael)	70	72	do.
Reculver (columns)	7	6	W. Marshall.
Ripon	151, 153, 155, 156	...	...
Rochester	7, 160	167	J. T. Micklethwaite.
Rodmersham	38		...
Rodney Stoke	109, 123	109	F. H. Crossley.
Rome, Old St Peter's	3	1	Raphael's Cartoon.
Do., St Clement's	3, 4	2	Alan Potter.
Do., St Maria in Cosmedin	4	2	F. Bond.
Rowston	131	130	W. Marshall.
Ryton	98		
St Alban's	4, 163	162	H. Bedford Pim.
Do. St Michael	129		
St David's (presbytery screen)	17	18	H. Bedford Pim.
Do. (quire screen)		155	do.
St Fiacre-le-Faouet		85	Camille Enlart.
St Gall			
St Margaret		112	A. Watkins.
St Paul's, Warden		99	A. Whitford Anderson
Salhouse			
Salisbury		...	...
Sandridge		28	A. Whitford Anderson
Sandwich, St Mary			...
Santon Downham		93	G. H. Tyndall.
Scarning		55	do.
Sedgebrook			
Sedgefield			
Shere			
Shoreditch			
Shoreham			
Sittingbourne			
Southacre			
South Shoebury			
South Walsingham			...
Southwell		169	H. H. Kemp in *Arch. Assoc. Sketch Book*.
Southwold (chancel screen)	48, 49, 73	46	H. Jenkins.
Do. (parclose)	48, 49	47	F. Bond.
Do.	48, 49	47	do.

INDEX LOCORUM

Place	Text.	Illustration.	Source.
Spalding		...	...
Sparsholt		92	W. Marshall.
Stamford St John		21	J. F. East.
Stanton Harcourt		168	W. Jolly.
Staverton	15, 66	108	F. H. Crossley.
Stebbing		31	E. Clapton.
Stockton		27	E. J. Pope.
Stoke-in-Teignhead		59	F. H. Crossley.
Stonegrave		97	F. H. Crossley.
Stratton			...
Strensham		140	Oscar Clark in *Bristol and Gloucester Arch. Journal.*
Strumpshaw	10	...	...
Swymbridge	28, 48, 66	61	F. H. Crossley.
Tattershall			
Taunton		...	...
Terrington St Clement		133	W. Marshall.
Thurcaston		...	
Thurlton		54	F. Bond.
Tilbrook		111	J. K. Colling.
Tilney All Saints			
Tintinhull			
Torcello Cathedral		5	F. Bond.
Totnes		33	F. F. Fox.
Trondhjem		31	Munch.
Tyre			
Urishay	10		
Walpole St Peter		57	G. H. Tyndall.
Walsoken		38	F. Bond.
Waltham			
Wandsworth			
Warfield			
Washfield		96	F. H. Crossley.
Do. (detail)		96	do.
Watlington		172	T. Garner.
Wells Cathedral			..
Do., St Cuthbert		134	F. H. Crossley.
Welsh Newton		130	A. Watkins.
Wenhaston Doom		124	W. N. Matthews.
Do. Church		150	H. Jenkins.
Westham		114	F. Bond.
Westminster Abbey			
Do., St Margaret's	39, 159		...
Westwell	8, 24, 34	23	H. Bedford Pim.
Whaplode	115	116	W. Marshall.
Whitby	149	148	do.
Wickhamford	131	129	H. Bedford Pim.
Wigan	123	...	...

Place.	Text.	Illustration.	Source
Wimborne			
Winchcombe		...	...
Winchester Cathedral			
Do., St Cross			
Do., St John's			
Wingerworth			
Wingfield		114	F. Bond.
Wingham			
Winterborne Abbas			
Do. St Martin			...
Wolborough		20	F. H. Crossley.
Wool			
Worcester		...	
Worstead (chancel screen)	48, 49, 75	50	F. Bond.
Do., (tower screen)	136	136	do.
Yarnton	99	97	J. F. East.
Yately	39		
Yatton	40, 68		
Yaxley	56	53	F. Bond.
York	119, 122, 139, 151, 156	154	H. M. Platnauer.

INDEX RERUM

AISLES, eastern bays, 11, 24
Altars, *minimum No. of*, 10; *in lofts*, 122, 153; *in nave*, 10, 151, 155, 161; *of screen*, 10; *recesses for*, 7, 11
Ambo, 9
Anglo-Saxon chancel arches, 7
Apertures over chancel arch, 34
Arch design in screens, 56, 59
Arches distorted, 117
Artistic value of screens, 12

BALDACHINO, 9
Bands in church, 145
Barrier screens, 49
Bench ends, 68
Blessed Sacrament, exposition of, 121
Book rest in loft, 119
Brittany, influence of, 87

Cancelli, 1
Cathedrals, quire screens in, 151, 155
Chancel arch, narrow, 10; omitted, 15; openings over, 34; triple, 7
Chancel screen, 159, 13
  ,,   ,, why open, 49
Chancels, why narrow, 10
Chapel screens, 22
Chestnut, 38
Church planning, 15
Ciborium, 9
Classical screens, 94, 98, 99
Collegiate churches, 151
  ,,   screens, 151, 156
Colonnade screens, 3
Colonnades, Anglo-Saxon, 7
Colour in screens, 75
Commandments, 131
Contracts, 40
Copyism, 41
Cornice, 48, 60, 77
Cornish church plans, 41
Cost, 39
Coving, 111
Cresting, 66, 137
Crucifix, *see* ROOD
Cusping, 56

FENCE screens, 165
Fifteenth-century work, 94
Flemish influence, 73, 87
Foreign screens, 86
Foreshortening, 13
Fourteenth-century work, 93
French influence, 87, 141

GALLERIES, 141
Geographical distribution, 36
Gesso, 73

HOME-MADE screens, 68

ICONOSTASIS, 9
Illegal destruction, 139
Inscriptions, 42
Italian influence, 73

JACOBEAN screens, 98, 99
Jesus altar, 161
Jubé, 109

LATERAL altars, 10
Lead ornaments, 56
Lectern in loft, 119
Lenten veil, 9
Lithic design, 43
Lofts destroyed or transposed, 137

MAGNITUDE of screens, 15
Makers of screens, 68
Monastic screens, 157
Monials, 39
Muntins, 39
Music in church, 141

NAVE altars, 151, 161
Naves, parallel, 15
Netherlands, influence of, 73, 87
Norman balustrade, 87
Norway, English influence in, 32

OPENINGS over chancel arch, 34
Organs in lofts, 123, 139
Origin of screens, 1, 8

Paintings on screens, 70
Parapets of rood loft, 4, 111, 119
Parclose screens, 4, 21
Parish churches, screens in, 13
Pews in lofts, 123
  ,, screened, 22
Piers cased, 117
Piscinas in lofts, 122
Planning of quires, 3
Plans of screens, 13
Preaching in loft, 121
Presbytery screens, 17
Projections of loft, 119
Pulpit in loft, 121
Pulpitum, 157, 159

QUIRE screen, 157, 159 ; *why solid*, 153 ; *constructional value of*, 153
Quires in lofts, 123

RAILINGS, altar, 1
Regulars, 157
Removal of screens, 73

,,   ; of loft,

99

USE of lofts, 119

VAMPING trumpet, 147
Vaulting, 43, 48, 111
Veil, 9
Vellum, 75
Village-made screens, 68

WALLED rood screens, 163
Western galleries, 141, 149
Welsh screens, 77
Window-tracery screens, 32
Windows near tympanum, 129
Wool, 94

Printed at THE DARIEN PRESS, *Edinburgh.*

Lightning Source UK Ltd.
Milton Keynes UK
UKOW05f1704211116

288208UK00025B/667/P